Bart Walton

Edited by Cathie Scott
Cover design by Gene Avery North and Paul Reynolds
Interior design and layout by Eric B. Randall

and has shown the way ever since.

Table of Contents

Chapter 9

A Higher Power 181

...reference to pilgrimage is in the *Rigveda*, circa 1,500 BCE.[1] Since that time, the whole of India has been crisscrossed with pilgrim routes, many of which are still in use today. The largest attended pilgrimage in the world is the *Kumbh Mela* in Uttar Pradesh where tens of millions gather to bathe in the confluence of three sacred rivers at an auspicious time determined by the position of the planets.

The tradition of pilgrimage is by no means confined to Hindus. Pilgrimage is at the root of every spiritual tradition—more so today than at any time in history. Jewish pilgrims visit the Holy Land in Israel. Christian pilgrims walk the Camino de Santiago in Europe. Muslim pilgrims attend the *Hajj* in Mecca. Buddhist pilgrims travel to Bodh Gaya, India, where the Buddha attained enlightenment. And in Japan, pilgrims walk the "Path of 88 Temples" on the Island

of Shukoku as their ancestors have done for more
than 12 centuries.

No one knows why or even when the practice began.
All we know for certain is that pilgrimage is
something humans do and have done throughout
history. The practice seems to be wired into the
human psyche, as a quest for healing or redemption
or simply as a means to give thanks to the Divine by
connecting with a sacred object or place.

The common element in all forms of pilgrimage is
the journey. The outward journey, however, is only
symbolic of the inward journey—a spiritual quest to
discover who we are and our place in the universe. In
this sense we are all pilgrims, as depicted by 17th
century writer John Bunyan in his classic allegory
The Pilgrim's Progress.[2]

Between 1960 and 1970, the convergence of two
unusual events brought this spiritual quest into the
forefront of American culture. First was the discovery
and spread of the psychedelic experience—a
temporary yet profound experience of transcendence
brought on by hallucinogenic drugs. Second was the
arrival of Hindu and Buddhist teachers, bringing their
traditional teachings and practices from the East.

The impact of these events seeped into every aspect of Western society, influencing music, art, social

during this period. And in a broader sense, it's the story of a whole generation who participated in the same quest.

The primary focus of this book is the spiritual quest itself. I've omitted events in my life that aren't relevant to this main theme. Also, I've arranged the chapters by subject matter. While the story does follow a loose time line, the chapters often overlap chronologically.

As I'm writing this introduction I can't help but wonder about you, the reader. Are you a spiritual seeker yourself? If so, I hope you'll discover new avenues for exploration. Or perhaps you'll find a shared experience or insight that previously you weren't able to put into words. Or you may find, as I have, that living in the question is more open, alive, and filled with possibility than any conceptual answer can be.

Even if you're not a spiritual seeker, you're welcome here. I hope this book will pique your curiosity and trigger an inquiry of your own. Who are we? Why are we here? What happens after we die? These questions don't belong to any particular group or belief system. They arise spontaneously out of our human nature. I urge you to nourish these questions and give them space to grow in your inner landscape. And above all, don't be in a hurry to find answers.

Endnotes – Introduction

[1] A. G. Gold and Vasudha Narayanan, "Pilgrimage," *Hinduism, Encyclopaedia Britannica*, February 2018, https://www.britannica.com/topic/Hinduism/Pilgrimage.

[2] J. Bunyan, *The Pilgrim's Progress* (Oxford University Press, December 2003).

Experience

This story begins in December 1969 in Lexington, Kentucky. I was home for Christmas break after my first semester at the University of Virginia. It was a Friday afternoon and I was walking down the street with my good friend W.L. Wilson. We were on our way to a Christmas party, looking very 1960s in our sport coats and ties.

The author, 1968

Joking and laughing as we made our way down the street, we wondered aloud whether any "pot" might be available at the party.

Kentucky was somewhat of a backwater in the 1960s and hallucinogenic drugs were not easy to come by. W.L. and I had smoked marijuana on the rare occasion and more powerful hallucinogens were just starting to appear on the scene. After hearing some of the horror stories that were circulating, we both decided to steer clear of any of the stronger drugs. But apparently, destiny had its own agenda.

As we walked down the street, we spotted a strange figure coming our way. He was tall and lanky, wearing bell-bottomed jeans, leather boots and a buckskin jacket with long fringe. His black hair was in Afro locks, arching in all directions like wild corkscrews. As he walked towards us, the bouncing hair and leather fringe undulated in perfect rhythm with his measured stride. We stopped and stood there, wide-eyed and dumbstruck in our clean-cut, prep school attire.

As he got closer, we realized it was Teddy, an old classmate from grade school. We greeted him like long-lost friends and without wasting any time, Teddy got right to the point. "Hey, I'd like to turn you on to some really great acid.[1] Wanna try it?" Without giving it a second thought, we said, "Sure." He produced a small bottle and carefully shook out two small tablets. "You're going to really like this stuff," he assured us.

We each swallowed a tablet on the spot, said our farewell, and Teddy went on his way up the street. The

Europe. Our traditional upbringing, the threat of nuclear holocaust, the music, the prosperity, the Vietnam War—all these things conspired to move the collective zeitgeist in a new direction, particularly for young people. We were all riding a wave and were so thrilled by the scenery that no one paid much attention to where we were heading.

This first experience with LSD was by far the most important event up to that point in my life. It opened the doors to an inner landscape vaster and more varied than anything I had ever seen in the outer world. During the next eight hours, W.L. and I were psychologically disassembled and reassembled multiple times. When it was all over, some of the pieces were missing or never quite fit the same as before. Dazed and starry-eyed, we'd been on our first LSD trip.

The First Trip

After swallowing the pill, nothing happened for quite a while and I began to wonder what all the fuss was about. Gradually, I started to notice a heightened sense of mental clarity. I thought to myself, "Okay, this is interesting." Then suddenly I was on a rocket, holding on for dear life. The acuity of my mind and senses increased exponentially and my ordinary experience of reality transformed into a hyper-reality. To borrow an analogy from Plato, it was as if I had lived in a dark cave all my life and was suddenly catapulted into the full light of day.

The simplest experience became a flood of information that could be assembled in a seemingly infinite variety of ways. A tabletop became a rich multidimensional landscape that was both wondrous and terrifying. Motes of floating dust revealed the miracle of levitation in three-dimensional space. Each sight, smell, touch, taste, and sound was internalized, producing endless sensations of form and texture. Each sensation merged into emotion and each emotion morphed into profound meaning.

A pair of shoes on the floor appeared as pure abstract form and color, surpassing any sculpture in its rawness and beauty. On another level, the shoes told an epic story of the places visited and miles traveled, all perfectly chronicled by the scuffmarks and dirt. On yet

My subjective experience became fluid. There was no sense of boundary between me and the outside world. My name and history, my likes and dislikes, even my memories were simply thoughts—things that I assumed and wore like clothing. I watched as these psychological garments unraveled into threads and floated away in spacious awareness. What remained was an intuitive sense of something deeper— something I couldn't put my finger on, something autonomous, transparent, primordial and bursting with potential.

Several times during the evening, W.L. and I tried to talk with each other. But our words fell out like bricks and made strange noises, like a record being played backwards. All we could do is laugh and stare in amazement at the extraordinary new reality unfolding around us. In the vernacular of the times, our minds were blown.

Swimming in the Deep End

When I returned to college in January, my life was on a new trajectory. I went through all the motions of attending classes and spending time with friends and family. From all appearances, my world was still intact. But I was a different person inside and didn't know how to relate to my former life. I had discovered a new world and wanted to explore it further. Over the next few months, I continued to experiment with LSD as well as two other drugs: psilocybin and mescaline.

During the 1960s and 1970s, the most common hallucinogenic drugs were LSD, psilocybin and mescaline. LSD is a synthetic derivative of the chemical *ergotamine*, from the fungus *ergot*. It was discovered accidentally in 1938 by Swiss chemist Albert Hoffman who, at the time, was searching for a migraine headache remedy. Psilocybin is a naturally occurring compound found in several varieties of mushrooms. Mescaline is a similar compound found in varieties of cacti, most notably peyote. Certain indigenous peoples have used psilocybin and mescaline in religious practices for thousands of years.

All these compounds produce similar mind-altering effects. But of the three, LSD is by far the most potent

compounds was British psychiatrist Humphry Osmond (1917-2004). In the late 1950s, Osmond discovered the remarkable benefits of LSD and mescaline in the treatment of alcoholism and other psychological disorders. It was Osmond who coined the term psychedelic, derived from the ancient Greek *psyche* and *delos* or "mind-revealing." His discoveries stirred a great deal of interest in the psychiatric community, and by the mid-1960s, hundreds of papers on the subject had been published in medical journals throughout the United Kingdom and North America.

Unfortunately, the eventual banning of these compounds made further study impossible. In retrospect, it was the unbridled use (and abuse) of these drugs by young people like me that brought about their legal prohibition and halted all research into their legitimate use. Only recently has Osmond's work in the use of these drugs started to reemerge in psychiatric research.[2]

These are powerful substances. In an ideal world, they would be used under the supervision of an experienced therapist or guide who would determine an appropriate dose and setting for each individual. During the 1960s and 1970s, almost no one followed these precautions. We used these drugs indiscriminately as a form of recreation, with more than a few casualties along the way.

At first, acquiring the drugs was a challenge and the quality was always questionable. Unscrupulous dealers would often pass off the popular diet drug Dexedrine (an amphetamine) as LSD. But eventually, I secured a reliable source of pharmaceutical-grade LSD—just one of the benefits of living in a college town with well-equipped laboratories.

The next few trips were amazing and profoundly insightful—a kaleidoscope of endless mental and sensual experiences. But as often happens for the novice user, the expansive nature of the experience became unnerving and painful subconscious impressions began to surface. Both these factors can trigger fear and paranoia and lead to a downward spiral—or what was commonly referred to among psychedelic users as a bad trip.

unlikely, I decided to stop using the drugs and count myself lucky that I hadn't ended up in the "white room," to borrow a phrase from a popular song of the day.[3] But once again, destiny stepped in and took the upper hand.

Enter Timothy Leary

Any account of psychedelic drugs would be incomplete without mentioning Timothy Leary, the most famous promoter and spokesperson for the LSD experience during the 1960s and 1970s.

In 1950, Leary earned a PhD in clinical psychology from the University of California at Berkeley. During the following years, he served as assistant clinical professor in medical psychology at the University of California, San Francisco, and director of psychiatric research at the Kaiser Family Foundation. In 1959,

Leary was invited to Harvard University to serve as a lecturer in clinical psychology. While at Harvard, he became interested in new treatment modalities, including the use of psychoactive compounds.[4]

In 1960, he traveled to southern Mexico with a colleague to study the use of psychedelic mushrooms in the religious practices of the indigenous Mazatec Indians.[5] It was on this trip that Leary first ingested psilocybin mushrooms and the subsequent experience dramatically changed the course of his life. He later told his colleagues, "I learned more about my brain and its possibilities and more about psychology in the five hours after taking these mushrooms, than I had in the preceding fifteen years of studying and doing research in psychology."[6]

When Leary returned to Harvard, he began the Psilocybin Project to study the effects of psilocybin on various subjects, from prisoners to seminary students. The most impressive results came from the Concord Prison Experiment,[7] which monitored the progress of prisoners both during their prison term and after their release. Prisoners who participated in the project had a recidivism rate of under 25 percent, which was remarkable compared to the average rate in the US of nearly 64 percent at that time.

Despite the impressive results, Harvard shut down the project and fired Leary, along with several of his

The publicity surrounding Leary and his dramatic departure from Harvard generated tremendous interest in psychedelic drugs throughout the world. Young people began experimenting with the drugs and were having profound experiences of unity—a sense of expansion and, at the same time, oneness with the universe. The more governments and institutions tried to suppress this new experience, the more fascinating it became.

Leary's stated mission was to get as many people as possible to "turn on, tune in, and drop out"—that is, to turn on to the psychedelic experience, tune in to the unity of all life, and drop out of conventional society, rooted in materialism, competition, and fear.[8] Leary believed that if enough people had this experience, the result would be a quantum leap in human evolution, ushering in a new age of love and cooperation and putting an end to violence, war and hunger. The problem with this theory is that when the drug wears off, users return to their previous state of mind and behavior. All that remains of the experience is a memory. And the memory of unity is not the same as unity itself.

I met Timothy Leary in 1985 in Seattle, Washington. We had a fascinating discussion about the LSD experience and his work at the time, which was time travel and extraterrestrial colonization. He was an iconoclast and, in my view, a genius. Like most geniuses, he generated an endless stream of ideas that ran the gamut from brilliant to pure nonsense. In the presence of genius, our role as ordinary people is to carefully pick out the gems and disregard the rest. In this respect, Leary's manual for taking LSD was one of his more brilliant contributions.

The LSD Manual

In winter 1970, I was introduced to Leary's book *The Psychedelic Experience,*[9] which was essentially a manual for the use of psychedelic drugs. The book was based on the *The Tibetan Book of the Dead*, otherwise known as *Bardo Thodol,*[10] an ancient Buddhist text first translated in 1927 by American

anthropologist W.Y. Evans-Wentz. Leary's coauthor in
this project was Richard Alpert, who later changed his
—

i nodol is a scriptural guidebook to be read aloud while
a person is dying and for several days after death. The
purpose of the text is to help the soul navigate through
the various after-death experiences and ultimately to
realize its highest potential in the afterlife. In addition,
by hearing the text read aloud, the soul will attain a
more favorable birth if reincarnation occurs. This
process is referred to as "liberation through hearing."

Leary understood the enormous value of verbal
instruction as an aid for anyone in transition from one
state of consciousness to another. More importantly,
he made the connection between actual physical death
and psychological or egoic death, which takes place
during the psychedelic experience. From this
perspective, he designed the manual to be read aloud
as a navigational tool during a psychedelic session in
the same way as the *Bardo Thodol* is read during the
process of dying. The manual also includes

instructions on how to prepare for a psychedelic session and how to recognize the various changes in consciousness as they occur.

Our ordinary sense of identity is based on our thoughts and feelings. It is purely a psychological construct with no basis in reality. During a psychedelic session, this construct begins to fall apart, and without proper guidance, the normal reaction is to resist this process and try to hold one's psychological identity together. This leads to confusion and fear, which can manifest as negative or wrathful hallucinations as the projection of our own inner conflicts. However, if we simply surrender to the process and allow our sense of identity to dissolve, the experience transforms into an ecstatic release from our own psychological prison. It's then possible to experience our true spiritual nature, which lies beyond the mind and personality.

Enlightenment

The books of Leary and Evans-Wentz introduced me to the idea of enlightenment, which at the time was a new concept in the West. In the East, enlightenment is an ancient idea rooted in cultural and spiritual traditions that go back thousands of years. It refers to the direct experience of one's essential spiritual nature

and the realization that the body, mind, and
personality are only temporary outward manifestations

I ne concept of enlightenment is also part a broader
understanding of a multilayered universe. Underlying
the outer physical world is a spectrum of increasingly
subtle spiritual dimensions. And deeper still, beyond
all form, is the unbounded field of pure consciousness,
or spirit.

In India, an enlightened sage is called a *jnani* (knower
of reality) or a *jivan mukti* (liberated soul). Often,
these sages follow in a long line of adepts and spiritual
masters going back thousands of years. In the West,
examples of enlightened sages are more rare, but
would include many saints of Christianity, Judaism
and Islam, as well as philosophers, mystics and poets
such as Socrates, Plato, Spinoza, Emanuel
Swedenborg, Rumi, and Walt Whitman.

Up until this point in my life, I was somewhat agnostic
and never really thought about God. The whole idea of

a supreme being running the universe from heaven seemed absurd. But now I was beginning to realize that it wasn't God that was the problem. It was the simplistic concept of God that I'd been taught as a boy. These new ideas of consciousness and spiritual enlightenment presented a multidimensional model of the universe and a new concept of God as the underlying consciousness and intelligence that permeates all levels of reality.

Just hearing about enlightenment and realizing the implications of humans living in higher states of consciousness was a spiritual awakening unto itself. In a similar way, the concept of a multidimensional universe resonated deeply inside of me and threw a whole new light on the meaning and purpose of life. Collectively, these ideas were like a time bomb that exploded in my awareness waking me from a long sleep.

Transcendence

The Psychedelic Experience provided exactly the kind of guidance I needed at a time when I was able to make use of it. After a couple of readings, I decided to try LSD again with the hope that I might break through the psychological barriers and experience the "clear light" of transcendental consciousness described in the book.

possible distractions or interactions with others for at least eight hours.

It was a beautiful spring day and I found a perfect location—a grassy clearing in the woods with scattered crocus blossoms and a running stream. Taking this as a good omen, I swallowed a sizeable dose of LSD and waited for it to take effect. Within about an hour, my sense of identity began to dissolve and the familiar fear began rising up in my abdomen. Reading aloud the instructions from the book, I gathered my courage, let go, and allowed myself to be swallowed by endless waves of feelings and sensations.

For an unknown period, there was a sublime peace and what I can only describe as pure awareness—not awareness of anything in particular, just awareness itself. It's not even that "I" was aware. The sense of "I" disappeared and only awareness remained. Even more amazing, this awareness was alive, blissful, and teeming with possibilities.

When I opened my eyes, I saw a new world. It was not the world I had known before of dead matter and empty space. All space, matter, and bodies were woven together into a seamless living whole. Existence itself was a glorious miracle, and the fact that I was conscious of it was a miracle within a miracle. The universe and everything in it were floating in what the ancient seers called *Satchitananda*—the unlimited spaciousness of existence, consciousness, and bliss.[11] This view seemed unfathomable and mysterious, and yet intimate and ever present—just behind the thin façade of my ordinary thinking mind.

There was something eerily familiar about the spiritual dimension when it opened to my awareness—as if the experience is wired into the human nervous system like love, beauty, and delight. The ancient scriptures and philosophies came alive and I understood them for the first time. At the same time, all my assumptions and cherished beliefs about life, truth, love, and God were shattered and replaced by an unspeakable, unknowable mystery.

As the drug wore off, the habitual patterns of my egoic mind reasserted itself and the living experience of ᴜᴜᴉᴛᴄᴜ ᶠᴀᴅ ᴜᴉᴄ

ᴄᴜᴜᴀᴜ ᴢᴜᴘ ᴜᴀᴛᴏ ᴛʜᴇ transcendent experience most of the time. But no matter how often this happened, when the drug wore off I found myself back in my ordinary state of mind, with all the same conflicts and neuroses that I had before.

I held onto the hope that if I just kept taking the drug, I might eventually become established in some higher state of consciousness. But this turned out to be an illusion. I was only repeating the same experience again and again. Whatever value can be gained from the psychedelic experience, I had pretty much gotten in the first 8 or 10 sessions. The roughly 50 sessions that followed added little to my understanding. I had to face the fact that genuine enlightenment must require something more than simply taking a pill. To borrow from a passage by Rumi, "I needed more grace than I thought."[12]

All these revelations forced me to make a break from psychedelic drugs and the culture surrounding them. In late spring 1970 at the age of 19, I stopped taking all drugs and vowed to find a more sane and traditional approach to spiritual development.

Despite the dangers and the many questions raised about the usefulness of these drugs, I'm glad that I had the experience and grateful to Timothy Leary and other psychedelic pioneers for their contributions. The transcendent experience showed me beyond any doubt that I am something more than a body—that my essential self is eternal and spiritual in nature and that all of life is interconnected within a spiritual matrix. Also, it showed me that enlightenment is a genuine experience and possibly the next important stage in human evolution. Temporary as they were, these experiences left lasting impressions that continue to guide me today.

A Pilgrimage Begins

After I made the decision to walk away from drugs, my life took on a new energy and direction. I knew that that no matter what happened in my life, the only questions worth asking were who am I, what is life, and why am I here? I had no interest in academic or intellectual theories. I wanted only the pure understanding that arises within from direct insight.

with strong resistance. My parents were terrified that I'd been brainwashed by some nefarious cult. It was impossible to explain that a new knowledge and energy had awakened within me and that this was an important part of who I was. As the American spiritual teacher Ram Dass observed, "If you think you're enlightened, go spend a week with your family."[13]

To be fair, I don't blame my family for being horrified by the changes that took place in me over the course of a few months. I was young and ill equipped to articulate what had happened. My behavior was immature, brash, and at times unhinged. Most of all, I was inexperienced in the art of living in two worlds— the world of ordinary consensus reality and the world of a mystic and a pilgrim. Wisdom comes from experience. And experience is often a succession of painful mistakes. I made plenty of them.

I eventually learned to have one foot in both worlds—
to play the role of a family member and student while
holding onto a private life inside myself. I felt alone
and uncertain as to how I could maintain this balance
for the rest of my life. Little did I know that a similar
transformation was happening in thousands of young
people around the world. If I had known, I would have
taken comfort in a sense of community with other
pilgrims who had embarked on a similar path.

Endnotes – Chapter 1

[1] "Acid" was a common street name for LSD in the United States during the 1960s and 1970s

[2] D. Martin, "Humphry Osmond, 86, Who Sought Medicinal Value in Psychedelic Drugs, Dies," *The New York Times*, February 22, 2004.

[3] J. Bruce and P. Brown (Cream), *White Room*; *Wheels of Fire* (Polydor, 1968).

[4] Wikipedia contributors, "Timothy Leary," *Wikipedia, The Free Encyclopedia*, https://en.wikipedia.org/w/index.php?title=Timothy_Leary&oldid=912224653 (accessed August 23, 2018).

[5] Wikipedia contributors, "Timothy Leary"

[6] Wikipedia contributors, "Timothy Leary"

[7] Wikipedia contributors, "Concord Prison Experiment," *Wikipedia, The Free Encyclopedia*;

https://en.wikipedia.org/wiki/Concord_Prison_Experiment
(accessed August 27, 2018).

The After-Death Experiences on the Bardo Plane (Oxford University Press, 1967, Fourth Edition, 2000).

[11] *Satchitananda* is a Sanskrit compound of three words: *sat, chit,* and *ananda*: literally existence, consciousness, and bliss. This term first appears in various Upanishads during the first millennium BCE.

[12] C. Barks and J. Moyne, "Dissolver of Sugar," *Open Secret, Versions of Rumi* (Boulder, CO: Shambhala Publications, 1999), 70.

[13] Ram Dass Quotes; https://www.ramdass.org/ram-dass-quotes/

Transcendental Meditation

By late spring 1970, I had made up my mind that psychedelic drugs were no longer useful on my spiritual quest. I knew that if I was going to progress, I had to find a healthier and more traditional approach. So I quit using all drugs including marijuana and alcohol.

Around the same time, I ran into an old classmate from high school—Lawrence "Gibby" Gibson, who was an accomplished athlete and the school's star pole-vaulter in 1968 and 1969. I hadn't seen him for over a year and was delighted to learn that we would now be fellow students at University of Virginia (UVA).

Gibby had recently returned from a three-month yoga retreat in upstate New York. As a part of his spiritual practice, he had become a vegetarian and was doing an hour of hatha yoga every morning. I was immediately attracted to this lifestyle and decided to adopt the same diet and daily routine, appointing Gibby as my mentor.

Aside from the obvious health benefits, these changes helped me cultivate discipline and cement the seriousness of my intent. Yet I felt they weren't enough to generate the kind of inner transformation I was seeking. I wanted a spiritual practice that was complete and linked to a tradition of enlightenment.

The notion of a spiritual practice is practically unknown in the West. If the term comes up at all, it refers to contemplation, prayer, and the study of scriptures. However, in the East, the tradition of spiritual practice, or *sadhana*, goes back thousands of years and includes a wide array of postures, breathing exercises, and meditation techniques. The goal of these practices is to bring the individual mind into alignment with universal consciousness. The concept of sadhana represented a radical departure from the religious upbringing of my childhood. Instead of dogmatic belief in mythic stories, the Eastern traditions offered practical technologies for the transformation of consciousness. I was captivated by this idea and wanted to learn everything I could about these ancient practices.

ᴜᴘᴇ̲ᴜ̲ᵤ̲ centers around the world. But I'm getting ahead of myself. To tell the whole story about how TM entered my life, I need to go back a few years.

The Seeds of Sadhana Are Planted

The first time I learned of TM and Maharishi was in spring 1968. I was a third-year student at Woodberry Forest, an all-male preparatory school on a remote farm in northern Virginia. At the time, I considered school a necessary evil and did only enough work to get by. With the exception of math and chemistry, the classes bored the life out of me. My grandmother used to say, "An idle mind is the devil's workshop." In my case, no truer words were spoken. Fortunately, the library was well supplied with newspapers and magazines from all over the world and this is where I spent most of my free time. One day, I picked up the current issue of *The Saturday Evening Post* and found

a feature article about Maharishi Mahesh Yogi and
TM.[1] What caught my eye the most was that the
Beatles had learned this meditation from the Maharishi.
For any young person at that time, this was an
impressive endorsement.

The article explained TM as a method of taking the
conscious awareness inward to the source of thoughts,
or what Maharishi called "Being." It went on to
describe this style of meditation as a simple and
natural technique that could be learned and practiced
by anyone. This really ignited my interest and I knew
immediately that I wanted to learn how to meditate. I
devoured the whole article, hoping to find some
instructions on how to begin the practice.
Unfortunately, the article gave out no details about the
practice itself. I was disappointed and felt cut off from
the outside world. Here I was, stuck in some backwater
while this Maharishi fellow was teaching meditation in
England. From my perspective, he may as well have
been teaching on the moon.

Two years later, I was a student at UVA. I had
upgraded from a remote outpost in the Piedmont of
Virginia to Charlottesville, a sleepy town about 28
miles to the southwest. I remember walking to class
one morning and passing through a covered walkway

on the university lawn. Glancing up, I saw a poster with a picture of Maharishi advertising an introductory

But I was already late for class and didn't have time to stop.

I tried to concentrate during class but couldn't hear a word the instructor was saying. All I could think about was Maharishi's

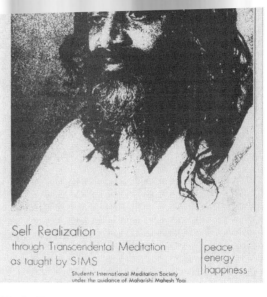

Self Realization
through Transcendental Meditation
as taught by SIMS   peace
                                     energy
       Students' International Meditation Society   happiness
       under the guidance of Maharishi Mahesh Yogi

Early Transcendental Meditation poster, circa 1970; courtesy of Paul Mason, http://www.paulmason.info/

picture and the possibility of learning his meditation technique. I never dreamed that TM would actually be available in Charlottesville. This was an incredible opportunity that I didn't want to miss. Only three or four times in my life have I been so absolutely certain about embarking on a new path. This was one of them.

After another 15 minutes, I gathered up my books and left the classroom. Retracing my steps, I began to look for the poster I had seen just 20 minutes earlier. To my disappointment it was gone. All that remained were three torn corners of paper still taped to the wall. I later learned that a student group of evangelical Christians ("Jesus freaks," as they were called in those days) considered meditation the work of Satan and were removing all the TM posters they could find.

Defeated for the moment, I immediately went to the library and combed through the card catalogue for books under "meditation." I found two entries: *Concentration and Meditation* by H. H. Swami Sivananda[2] and *The Science of Being and Art of Living,* by Maharishi Mahesh Yogi.[3] I checked out both books, and for the next two days, I could hardly put them down. Both authors explained meditation in much the same way. They both emphasized that meditation could be learned only through personal instruction from a qualified teacher. I felt disappointed but also determined to obtain this instruction and begin the practice.

For the next several weeks, I was obsessed with a single purpose—to find out how I could learn

know about meditation, and even better, he pointed out his apartment building and told me his name—Preston Thomas. On the spot, I went to Preston's apartment and knocked on the door. A tall, lanky guy answered. I asked, "Do you know anything about meditation?" He said, "Yeah, come on in." That turned out to be the beginning of a lifelong friendship.

Preston was a graduate student in philosophy at UVA. He was writing a PhD dissertation on the work of Baruch Spinoza, a 17th century Dutch philosopher regarded as one of the fathers of the 18th century Enlightenment. Preston had completed the class requirements and had four years to write his dissertation. He used this time primarily to meditate, watch Star Trek reruns, and occasionally take LSD if the *I Ching* predicted an auspicious journey.

Preston had two roommates at the time. The four of us became good friends and I began hanging out at Preston's apartment during all my spare time. Preston was a philosopher in the truest sense of the word. Also, he was older than the rest of us and more advanced in esoteric knowledge and spiritual development. We all looked up to him.

Preston's apartment was retrofitted with floor-to-ceiling bookshelves containing a comprehensive library of philosophical and esoteric books from around the world. In 1970, this was a rare find almost anywhere but especially in Charlottesville, Virginia.

In addition, Preston's room had a state-of-the-art speaker system. His desk was equipped with a panel of switches, allowing him to control the lights, music, radio, fan, air conditioner, and television. He could even mute the television commercials with the press of a button. Preston sat at his desk in a reclining chair, mostly in the dark, meditating and listening to the ocean from a recording of environmental sounds. His room had an ambiance of stillness and sacredness. We didn't really know what was going on but sensed that Preston was an advanced being in a special category of his own. We were always careful to maintain a certain hushed reverence whenever we entered his room.

program in Charlottesville. After searching diligently for two weeks, I had finally struck pay dirt.

As it turned out, the regional TM teacher was just beginning a course of instruction in Charlottesville. Although I had missed the introductory lecture, I learned that I could attend a second lecture that evening and catch up. This was good news. It meant that I wouldn't have to wait another six months for the teacher to return to town.

When evening arrived, I walked from my dorm to the lecture at the Student Union building. The teacher was a handsome fellow in his late 20s named Lew Leonard. I don't remember much about the lecture, but I do remember that Lew seemed relaxed and had a charming sense of humor. I was already familiar with the main points about TM and how it worked from reading Maharishi's book. After the lecture, I stayed behind with about eight others who wanted to sign up for the four-day training scheduled to begin the next day.

The Origins of TM

For those who may not know much about Maharishi and TM, I'll provide some historical context.

Very little is known about Maharishi's birth family or upbringing. In keeping with monastic tradition, he never spoke about himself or his early life. By most accounts, he was born Mahesh Prasad Varma on January 12, 1917, in Jabalpur, India. His family was a member of the *Kayastha* caste, which traditionally is reserved for professional writers, scribes, and keepers of public records.[4]

Maharishi's guru was a spiritual luminary of North India named Swami Brahmananda Saraswati, affectionately known by his disciples as Guru Dev. After leaving home at the age of nine, Guru Dev spent most of his life in solitude, meditating in remote jungles and forest caves. Despite his efforts to remain anonymous, people from all walks of life flocked to receive his *darshan*, or blessing, whenever he ventured into towns and villages.

In 1941, the Indian Religious Federation persuaded
Guru Dev to come out of seclusion and accept the seat
of Shankaracharya of Jyotir M...

...ly recognized his stature as a
spiritual master. When Mahesh asked to become a
disciple, Guru Dev told him to first complete his
studies at Allahabad University. After he graduated in
1942 with a BS degree in physics, he joined Guru Dev
as a novice monk and was given the name Bal
Brahmachari Mahesh. He was initially assigned various
menial jobs in the ashram. Over time, he rose in rank
to become Guru Dev's chief secretary and
spokesperson.

According to legend, at some point before his death,
Guru Dev gave the teachings of TM to Maharishi and
told him to make it available to the general public. In
later years, Maharishi said that TM was an ancient
practice from the Vedic tradition that Guru Dev revived
in order to raise global consciousness.

After Guru Dev's death in 1953, Maharishi went into seclusion near Rishikesh in North India. Several years later, he felt an inner calling to travel to South India, where he was asked to give a series of lectures. The response to his talks was overwhelming and with this initial encouragement, Maharishi decided to spread the practice of TM around the world.

Maharishi's life as a spiritual teacher extended over 50 years, from 1955 to his passing in 2008. He revived many ancient teachings from the Vedic tradition, of which TM was the foundation and by far the most important. Throughout his life, Maharishi was one-pointed in purpose and consistently gave credit for his teachings to Guru Dev.

Initiation

I took formal instruction in TM on a cold Saturday in March 1970. From that first day, I knew that meditation would play an important role in my life. It's not that I had a profound experience in the beginning—far from it. I just knew this was the right path for me and I committed myself to the daily practice. The psychedelic experience had given me a glimpse of the possibilities. But now I wanted a traditional practice to cultivate my spiritual experience. I trusted that TM would be the answer.

.....y. we meditated together a few times to make sure that I had the hang of it, and then I meditated alone in another room for about 15 minutes. That was all for the first day. For the next three evenings, all the new meditators met together for a group meditation, a short talk about correct practice, and then questions and answers about our experiences.

The first few years of meditation were fairly uneventful. I often felt discouraged because nothing seemed to be happening. At times I thought that meditation was too slow or just wasn't working for me. Despite these initial doubts, I was regular in my practice and didn't give up.

One reason I wasn't having a good experience in the beginning may have been my past drug use. During the TM introductory lecture, people are advised to abstain from recreational drugs for at least two weeks prior to instruction. In my case, however, two weeks was probably not long enough. I think it took me several years to recover from more than 60 LSD trips. Another reason was that I wasn't meditating correctly. In my eagerness to progress, I developed the habit of concentrating on the mantra, which is counterproductive and inhibits the process of meditation.

Despite these impediments, something wonderful would occasionally happen. Without any effort or intention, the floor would seem to fall away and I would disappear into pure consciousness—fully awake but in a state of mental and physical equilibrium. In TM language, this experience is called, "transcending." I would come out of these meditations feeling rejuvenated and with a renewed dedication to the practice.

TM as a Practice

TM is a form of mantra meditation, which is a common spiritual practice in the East, going back thousands of years. Mantras are traditional Sanskrit words, or sounds, representing different aspects (names) of the Divine—what Maharishi called "impulses of creative intelligence." Mantras are traditionally used in ritual worship as well as recitation of scripture. More importantly, they are used in various forms of spiritual

̇ ̇ ̇ ̇ ̇ ̇ ̇ ̇ ̇ ̇ ̇ ̇ ̇ ̇ ̇ ̇ ̇ ̇ of *japa*, or

the instructions on how to use it correctly,
core and substance of TM and something that is not
easily conveyed through oral or written instruction. It's
a bit like learning to ride a bicycle. Oral instruction
plays a role but only up to a point. After that, the
student must gain direct experience, or the feel of
correct and effortless meditation.

The point of meditation is for individual awareness to
relax into the field of pure consciousness, which lies
beyond the thinking level of the mind. Anyone who has
tried to meditate knows that effort is counterproductive
because it holds the awareness on the active thinking
level. And yet, without any effort at all, the mind
wanders aimlessly and meditation never happens.
From this perspective, effort is both an impediment
and a necessary component of correct meditation.
This conundrum has been a major hurdle for
meditators since the beginning of time.

The genius of TM is that the student is not told how to meditate but rather is led into the experience of correct meditation through a series of steps. In this respect, Maharishi's TM instruction is brilliant and unique among the different forms of meditation available today. I speak from experience as someone who has experimented with many different forms of meditation from various traditions around the world.

Transcending

Trying to describe transcending is like trying to explain color to a blind person. Nevertheless, I've found that many people have had the experience to some degree and may not have been aware of it. It can happen spontaneously or be triggered by different physical conditions or external stimuli. The experience can vary widely from person to person, both in terms of clarity and frequency.

This is what transcending is like for me. During meditation mental activity slows down. Some thinking continues but is very faint and seems to be going on by itself in the background. The mind is awake and alert but in a state of rest. If the experience is clear and continues to deepen, a profound sense of peace, clarity, and inner happiness arises without any ˢ ᴵ ᵗʳʸ to locate or analyze the

˜ ᵗʰᵉ peace

As an analogy, oui ᵤ.ᵤ..

compared to a wave on the ocean. Certaiₙ ᵢᵥ. ˍ

converge for a wave to appear. As soon as those
forces dissipate, the wave loses its individuality and
merges back with the ocean. The experience of
transcending is like that—the merging of individual
mind with the ever-present ocean of nonlocal
consciousness that underlies everything.

Transcending can be a clear experience or something
vague and indistinct. The effects of transcending
extend beyond the period of meditation. Even a few
moments of the experience are deeply restful for the
body and mind. On the psychological level, the
experience fills me with a sense of peace and meaning
that may last for days.

The Nature of Consciousness

No one really knows what consciousness is. Even neuroscientists refer to consciousness as the "hard problem" because it can't be explained through normal reductive science. This is because consciousness is not an object of perception. Rather, it's the subjective reality behind the mind that makes perception possible. Trying to understand consciousness is like the eye trying to see itself. However, in some paradoxical way, when consciousness is not outwardly directed, it can recognize itself. In this recognition is the discovery of our own essential nature.

Three important insights arise from this recognition. (By insight, I mean the direct realization of a self-evident truth.) The first insight is that we are not our thoughts. When the awareness disengages from thinking, thoughts are seen as impulses that arise and fall away spontaneously, shaped by our individual conditioning and destiny.

The second insight is that our essential nature is not located in time or space. Our thinking mind is associated with our body and personality. But because we can observe these things, they can't be who or what we really are. In some fundamental way, we are free and not bound by these associations. Another way to put it is that our true self is spiritual in nature and

~~~~~~~~~~~~~~~~~~~~lately different

separateness without question. But the experience of
transcending reveals a radically new perspective. At
the most fundamental level of life, consciousness is
universal and indivisible. As an analogy, consider a
cluster of islands in the ocean. On the surface, they
appear to be individual and separate. But at deeper
levels, they're all connected as one landmass. In this
same way, all sentient beings are connected in
universal consciousness.

The ancient sages of India referred to this universal
consciousness as *Satchitananda*, or being, intelligence,
and bliss.[5] In the Tibetan Buddhist tradition, it is
described as the Great Perfection—"a pristine, clear,
awake and bare freshness, which has never changed."[6]
Maharishi used many names for it, such as being, the
absolute, the transcendent, pure consciousness, the
home of all knowledge, the field of all possibilities, and
the unified field.

Progress in Meditation

My first clear experience of transcending happened
several months after I learned to meditate. It impressed
me so deeply that I still remember the place, season of
the year, and even details of the room where I was
sitting. Having such a deep experience without the aid
of drugs filled me with a sense of freedom along with
the certainty that I was on the right path. Unfortunately,
this experience was a rare event during those early
years and the long dry spells in between were
discouraging and often boring.

After I had been meditating for several years, I noticed
changes that came in distinct stages. While meditating,
something inside me would let go—a tension that I
didn't even know existed. In some subtle way, this
tension had been inhibiting the process and when it
dissolved, a deep feeling of relaxation would ripple
through my whole being. Often this relaxation would
be accompanied by the clear realization that I now
understood how to meditate correctly for the first time.

I would get used to this new level of practice for
several months, and then I would fall into a deeper
relaxation and an even clearer understanding of
correct practice. After moving through dozens of these
stages, I realized that progress in meditation is

measured not only in terms of relaxation but also in terms of a deeper understanding of correct practice

perhaps it was just the right time in terms of my overall development. In any event, daily meditation practice took on a new meaning and importance in my life.

Looking back as a 50-year practitioner, I consider it to be a stroke of good luck that I learned TM at a time in my life when I was able to commit to a daily practice. Moreover, I'm grateful that I continued with the practice during those early years when my experience was often flat and uninteresting.

Advanced Courses and Teacher Training

In summer 1972, I attended a month-long TM meditation course called The Science of Creative Intelligence (SCI) at Queens College in Kingston, Ontario, Canada. At the time, Maharishi was trying to legitimize TM in the West and avoid any associations with mysticism or religion. He wanted people to think of TM as a practical technique that anyone could use regardless of their religious beliefs or cultural background. SCI was his attempt to explain the mechanics of consciousness, meditation, and human development in scientific terms.

During the course, we were given instruction in yoga *asanas*, or postures, and *pranayama*, or controlled breathing exercises. We were told to add these practices to our regular 20-minute meditation. These three practices in sequence constituted one "round," and the daily practice of multiple rounds was referred to as "rounding." We were instructed to gradually increase the number of rounds as the course progressed.

By the time we got up to eight rounds per day, people started having unusual experiences, ranging from extended states of deep transcending to profound physical and emotional releases. From my own experience and observations of others, I began to appreciate the profound impact these practices have on the mind and physiology.

I also learned the importance of following the "rounding" instructions to the letter. One incident that I recall underscores this point. One of the participants in particular lived a few doors down the hall in my

I peeked in as I was walking by. He was meditating naked in full lotus posture on a deerskin. I thought that was a little strange but decided to mind my own business and I walked on to my room.

A couple of days later, I heard a lot of shouting and commotion in the hallway. I opened my door and saw him strapped to a gurney being rolled down the hallway by an emergency response team. This was a classic example of someone who decided that if a little meditation is good, then a lot of meditation is even better. Instead of rounding as instructed, he was meditating for extended periods without breaks for meals or exercise.

In fall 1973, I took the next step in my involvement with TM and attended a six-month teacher-training course, which took place in an off-season ski resort just outside of Lenzerheide, Switzerland. There were about 90 participants in my group, mostly young people from the US. Overall, the program was well designed and well conducted. For six blissful months, our routine consisted of multiple rounds of yoga, pranayama, and meditation combined with a couple of hours of study each day. I enjoyed the long periods of meditation as well as the advanced training. But most of all, I enjoyed long evenings with Maharishi in small groups of 20 to 30 people. He was very accessible in those days and I took full advantage of every opportunity to be with him whenever possible.

Maharishi Mahesh Yogi (1918-2008),
Seelisberg, Switzerland, circa 1972

A Crack in the Coherence

(In until about 1975 the TM

...heavy bureaucracy descended over
every aspect of its operations. The original collective
spirit of love, service, and fellowship became
overshadowed by internal politics and grabs for power.
I don't know if this was Maharishi's fault or the result of
a burgeoning organization and the inevitable
corruption that comes with success and rapid
expansion.

As much as I enjoyed the long meditation courses and
my association with Maharishi, I frequently clashed
with the TM culture during those years. The way we
were taught to engage with the public was scripted and
artificial, without room for innovation or initiative on
the part of the teacher. Maharishi's judgment was
considered absolute and infallible. The unspoken rule
was to accept without question whatever Maharishi or
the movement leadership said.

As the organization continued to grow in the 1980s, so did my frustration with the authoritarian bureaucracy. During one meditation course, I was reprimanded for reading a newspaper. Apparently, a decision had been handed down from global headquarters that we should not be exposed to any negative news during courses. My newspaper was confiscated, and I was told to read the *Age of Enlightenment News*, a photocopied summary of the positive events of the week. Exasperated, I let loose with some choice words about the *Age of Enlightenment News* and what they could do with it.

I found out later that the incident was reported up the food chain. I was labeled "a crack in the coherence" and blacklisted, which meant that I was barred from attending future meditation courses. This was a painful event compounded by the fact that I had no recourse to appeal or even tell my side of the story. But with the passage of time, I realized that this experience liberated me from the TM culture and allowed me to reorient my life according to my own destiny. Looking back, I'm grateful that it happened exactly as it did.

When I think about my experiences with the TM organization during those years, I'm reminded of a passage from *The Caine Mutiny* by Herman Wouk:

"The Navy is a master plan designed by geniuses for execution by idiots. If you are not an idiot, but find

their business and spiritual objectives. As far as I know, the blacklist has been abolished and the rules for participation on meditation courses have been relaxed considerably.

Maharishi as a Spiritual Master

Like my relationship with the TM organization, my relationship with Maharishi was complex and full of contradictions. How does one separate Maharishi from the organization he founded and managed on a day-to-day basis? Yet somehow, in my mind, I managed to do just that and, to some extent, still do.

I clearly remember the first time I met Maharishi. It was in fall 1973 during my teacher-training course in Switzerland. One morning at breakfast, one of my friends on kitchen staff whispered to me that Maharishi would be arriving that afternoon. I immediately saw an opportunity to meet Maharishi in person without a lot of people crowding around. I waited until late afternoon when most people were in their rooms. Then I snuck down to the kitchen, filled a small basket with fruit and flowers, and waited near the front door for Maharishi's arrival.

Waiting patiently is not something that I do well, but on this occasion, I stood and waited for over two hours. Finally, a car drove up. Two guys in suits opened the passenger door and Maharishi stepped out. I was a completely taken aback by his diminutive stature—five feet tall at the very most. I somehow imagined him much larger. But then when he walked into the hotel, I was struck by the sudden contrast. The power of his presence was enormous, as if an elephant had just walked into the lobby.

While his attendants were busy unloading the luggage, Maharishi turned, looked in my direction, and walked over to me. This was completely unexpected because I was standing off to the side, trying to be as inconspicuous as possible. He looked directly at me and said, "Hmm?" Although there were no words, I clearly heard him asking, "You have something for me?" Dumbstruck, I must have looked like a deer in the headlights. Finally, I said, "Oh yes, Maharishi, I have some things for you to take to your room." He just looked at me for a few moments and didn't say a word as he took the small basket. I was sure that I

heard, "Come on." I hopped into the elevator and rode with everyone up to the top floor. Maharishi exited first and took off down the hall while his attendants scrambled with the luggage and tried to keep up. I was following behind when one of the attendants blocked me and suggested I must have other things to do. I tried to hang around for a while, but it was clear that I wasn't going to get into Maharishi's room. So I gave up and went to my own room.

For the next couple of days, I was a bit stunned. I had no doubt that as soon as Maharishi saw me in the lobby, he knew that I wanted to speak to him. He could easily have ignored me and walked on to the elevator. Instead, he responded to my silent request. Even more amazing was how he communicated clearly and effortlessly without speaking. This was my first encounter with Maharishi and with his *siddhis*, or yogic powers.

As I later learned, Maharishi had a number of these unusual abilities. What most people would consider supernatural or miraculous were everyday events around Maharishi. They were so common, in fact, that everyone just took them as a matter of course. For example, a much-needed person or resource would show up at just the right moment. Projects that seemed impossible or doomed to failure would miraculously come together at the last minute. Maharishi would know about events happening at a far distance without being informed through normal means. It was impossible to hide anything from him as I experienced personally on more than one occasion.

I'll give one example, which occurred during a six-month advanced course that Anne and I attended in France. We were not married at the time, and the unmarried men and women were segregated in different hotels. One night, I snuck out of my hotel and hitchhiked to a neighboring town to spend the night with Anne. The next day I hitchhiked back to my hotel and crept into my room without being noticed. This was completely off the program and I would probably have been sent home if the course leaders had found out. The next day, Maharishi asked me how things were going. I'm embarrassed to confess that I'm a pretty good liar and, on this occasion, I gave it my best shot. But as Maharishi was looking at me, his expression suddenly changed. He put hand to his

Maharishi never made a show of these abilities, nor did he try to hide them. He attributed them to the "support of nature" and said they happen naturally when the mind falls into alignment with Cosmic Intelligence.

The human mind will struggle to rationalize these kinds of events or try to find ways to deny that they happened. After witnessing them again and again, I learned to accept them as a matter of fact. My sense is that these powers were not something he tried to cultivate. They simply came with the territory, as part of the immense energy that surged through him. My time with Maharishi helped me realize that there really are no supernatural events; there are only natural events, some of which we cannot yet understand or explain.

Setting aside the notion of siddhis, Maharishi was extraordinary in many other ways. For example, he slept only three or four hours a night. When awake, he appeared to be connected to an inexhaustible supply of energy and happiness that informed his mind and directed his speech and actions. Everyone around him received an indirect surge of this power along with a glimpse of its strength and depth. He saw the good in everyone and the humor in every situation. His frequent laughter was infectious and charmed everyone within earshot.

Maharishi radiated enormous charisma and *shakti*, or spiritual power. Whenever I was with him, the incessant chatter in my mind came to a stop, leaving a spacious awareness where every word out of his mouth landed like holy scripture. If I had a list of questions, I forgot about them or they just didn't seem to matter anymore. Everyone who spent time with Maharishi had a similar experience. Those who knew him and personally experienced the power of his presence had no doubt that he was a spiritual master and that he had a genuine calling to raise the consciousness of the world.
Despite his enormous energy and charisma, Maharishi was not infallible. Yet taking everything into account, he was an extraordinary man and his

accomplishments speak for themselves. Under his direction, thousands of meditation centers were

I received other priceless gifts from Maharishi. For example, I learned the value of looking for the good in every situation. I distinguish this from positive thinking because it's not about thinking. It's the recognition that at its deepest level, life is good and beautiful regardless of how it may appear on the surface. The negative or pessimistic view is almost always a narrow interpretation of reality. By looking for the good and the beautiful, we expand our perspective and align ourselves with life at its most fundamental level.

This view may seem simplistic and naïve, but actually it's a profound spiritual teaching that Maharishi didn't talk about so much as he demonstrated in the way that he lived day to day. In the heat of the moment, I'm not always able to put this teaching into practice. Yet next to meditation, it strikes me as the most important of his teachings and the most practical in its application.

Finally, Maharishi gave me, and many like me, an important role model that we desperately needed as young people in the 1960s and 1970s. He was a man of great vision and energy with a one-pointed objective—to bring about the spiritual regeneration of the world. Maharishi held himself and his mission in high esteem, yet he remained humble and gave all the credit for his accomplishments to Guru Dev. He demonstrated profound silence, combined with inner strength, focus, and dynamism. And most importantly, he always maintained a childlike sense of humor.

I believe that to a large extent, the people who make the biggest impressions on us determine who we become. In this respect, Maharishi played an enormous role in my spiritual growth and development as a human being.

Endnotes – Chapter 2

[1] "There Once Was a Guru from Rishikesh,"*Saturday Evening Post*, May 4, 1968, p 25, Curtis Publishing Co.

[2] H.H.S. Sivananda, *Concentration and Meditation*, Second Edition (Divine Life Society, Second Edition, 1959).

[3] M.M. Yogi, *The Science of Being and Art of Living* (Delhi, India, Allied Publishers, Pvt., Ltd., 1963), current edition (Fairfield, IA: MUM Press, 2011).

[4] Wikipedia contributors, "Maharishi Mahesh Yogi," *Wikipedia*

[6] H.H. Dudjom Rinpoche, *Extracting the Quintessence of Accomplishment* (Darjeeling, India: Ogyan Kunsang Choekhorling, 1979).

[7] H. Wouk, *The Caine Mutiny* (New York: Doubleday and Company, 1952), Ch. 9

Plato

Plato has played an important role in my spiritual journey—not only during my youth but throughout my adult life and especially now as I approach old age. How did this happen? Plato is not exactly easy reading and I'm certainly no scholar—far from it.

I first learned about Plato in high school, but it wasn't until my freshman year at college that I made a serious effort to study his work. One of the first dialogues that I read was the *Apology*—an account of Socrates' trial in 399 BCE and his response to the charges brought against him. At one point, I was so overcome that I broke down and cried. Never has a book affected me this deeply. His words are radical and defiant yet without a hint of anger or ill will. At the same time, they convey the highest ideals of the human spirit.

Perhaps my experience with LSD and meditation prepared me for Plato's teaching. In any event, his essential message resonated deeply with me. One of my lifelong ambitions has been to share this message with others. Now, some 45 years later, I've decided to give it my best effort. I owe that much to Plato.

Historical Background

Not a great deal is known about Plato's early life. He was born in Athens around 428 BCE to an aristocratic family that was influential in the social and political affairs of the day. He received the best education available, including grammar, mathematics, music, gymnastics, and philosophy. His teachers praised him for his modesty and for being a quick study.

Plato, 427-347 BCE.[1]

At the same time, he excelled in athletics and distinguished himself in wrestling at the Isthmian games.[2] His likenesses often show evidence of the broken nose he received during those matches.

By one account, Plato's given name was Aristocles, after his maternal grandfather. His wrestling coach

and he was known as Plato ever since.

As a young man, Plato aspired to a career in politics. However, two significant events changed the course of his life and reshaped his attitudes about human nature and social order. The first was a series of blunders made by the Athenian rulers during the Peloponnesian Wars. As a result, Athens came under the rule of neighboring Sparta and the cherished Athenian democracy was replaced by an oligarchy of 30 tyrants. The second, and perhaps more painful event for Plato, was the trial and execution of his beloved friend and teacher Socrates.

For decades, Socrates had been outspoken and relentless in his mission to expose ignorance and hypocrisy wherever he found it. He made enemies among the Athenian ruling class, many of whom wanted him eliminated. But how? Even though he was a thorn in their side, he had not broken any laws. Then, during the Peloponnesian Wars, one of Socrates' students committed treason. This created the perfect pretext for the authorities to arrest Socrates for blasphemy and for corrupting the youth, charges that carried the death penalty. The trial was a sham; the guilty verdict was a *fait accompli*.

It was customary in such cases for the condemned prisoner to plead for a lighter sentence, such as exile, which was usually granted. But with his characteristic irony, Socrates argued that instead of punishment he should be rewarded for his valuable service to the state. He proposed that he be given free dining at the *Prytaneum*, where victorious athletes were showered with honors after the Olympic games. The judges were not amused. The death sentence was upheld and, one month later, Socrates was executed by means of poison hemlock.

These events affected Plato deeply and made him pessimistic about the possibility of a just state. Moreover, they reinforced his views about human nature and political power—that those who crave power are unfit to rule and, conversely, those most fit to rule have no desire for power. This conundrum created the perfect setting for Plato's realization that our highest ideals of goodness, truth, justice, and beauty do not exist in the earthly realm. The quest to

returned to Athens and started the world's first university (the Academy) where he instructed the great minds of his day. Many of his students went on to become renowned rulers, philosophers, theologians, mathematicians, architects, and teachers throughout the ancient world. Plato continued to oversee the Academy until his death in 347 BCE at the age of 80.

Plato's Place in History

Plato's contribution to Western civilization is immense. The fact that his entire body of work—some 30 books written almost 2,000 years before the printing press—has survived intact is a testament to his enduring legacy. Up until the 20th century, his dialogues served as the foundation for studies in drama, literature, mathematics, cosmology, theology, political science, and philosophy. In 1929, British mathematician and philosopher Alfred North Whitehead wrote, "The safest general characterization of the European philosophical tradition is that it consists of a series of footnotes to Plato."[4]

Plato's most important book *The Republic* was the first philosophical work to tackle practical questions about how to live in the world, both individually and collectively. It probes deeply into the nature of reality, knowledge, and ethics, as well as social and political order. Throughout the book, one recurring question seems foremost on Plato's mind: What is a good life and how do we live it?

To address this question, Plato leads us through a series of questions: What is a human life? What is justice and why should we behave justly? What is the benefit of virtue over the mere appearance of virtue? What is the highest good in life and how can we align ourselves with it? And finally, What is the nature of the soul and does it survive the death of the body? In Plato's view, all these questions are interrelated and informed by ideals that shine into the human psyche from higher dimensions of reality.

What emerges from these inquiries is a political and moral order that is comprehensive, and yet so radical and unsettling that we can only conclude—as Plato did himself—that the ideal state is not possible in this world. Nevertheless, our attempt to construct it in our

spiritual pursuits didn't exist during Plato's time. The ancient Greek word *philosophia* means the love or pursuit of wisdom. It suggests a quest for truth in all areas of life. Plato wasn't interested in mere abstract theories. He wanted to know in very practical terms what constitutes a good life and how to live it. He wasn't afraid to dive into the hard questions about life, death, love, truth, and reincarnation. Using his unique style of dialectic, he followed these inquiries wherever they led. When he ran up against the limits of reason and language, he wasn't afraid to leap into the unknown and the ineffable.

Modern scholars have never been completely comfortable with Plato. On one hand, they can't really ignore him. He's been considered the founder of Western philosophy for over 2,400 years. His dialogues are too brilliant to be dismissed. On the other hand, he keeps dropping hints of something wonderful and mysterious beyond reason and understanding and it's these references that often make modern philosophers squirm. For example, when Socrates hears the voice of his spirit guide warning him that he's about to make a mistake, or when he talks about the afterlife and reincarnation, or even more bizarre, when he goes into a trance-like state, leaving his companions baffled and confused.

When I was studying Plato in college, my professors would either ignore these passages or invent far-fetched interpretations to explain them away. Eventually, I realized that there's a fundamental difference between the modern approach to philosophy and where Plato is leading us in his dialogues. My professors seemed interested only in an intellectual dissection of Plato's writings. They weren't curious to look where Plato is pointing, to participate in his inquiry, and through this process, to discover something new. Beneath the surface of these dialogues, Plato is inviting us to make a leap from thinking and believing to seeing and knowing for ourselves.

Plato's Teaching

The essence of Plato's teac~~~~~ ~ ~ ~ ~

~~~~~~~~~~ projected onto a wall by the light of
a fire behind them. Their whole experience of reality is
based on shadow images because this condition of
bondage is all they've ever known.

Free men (teachers) from the upper world frequently
descend into the cave to help the prisoners break free.
But this is not an easy task. The cave is dark and the
deafening echoes make it difficult to think or
communicate. The teachers try to explain to the
prisoners that the images on the wall are mere
shadows and that in the real world above, actual
objects are three-dimensional and can be seen in the
full light of day. But to the prisoners, these stories
seem unbelievable if not completely insane.

A teacher is sometimes successful in helping some of
the prisoners loosen their chains and see for
themselves how the shadows are being projected onto
the wall. The shock of this experience is traumatic,

causing them to panic and thrash out. Despite the difficulties, the teacher manages to free one or two of the prisoners and drag them, kicking and screaming, out of the cave and into the light of day.

At first the newly freed prisoners are blinded by the daylight. Gradually they're able to see real objects and then to look up and behold the sun as the source of all light and perception. As the newly freed prisoners begin to comprehend this new knowledge, they can't imagine ever returning to the state of ignorance and bondage that they endured in the cave. But the teacher points out that with knowledge comes responsibility to serve others. Out of a sense of duty, they agree to return to the cave to help their fellow prisoners gain freedom. In this way the knowledge of truth is passed from one generation to the next.

In this allegory, Plato depicts the human condition as one of bondage and our experience of the world as a projection that occurs in the mind from the dim light of our senses. To comprehend the reality behind this projection, we need the help of a teacher who can lead us step by step from beliefs and opinions to understanding, then to intuition, and finally to insight and the direct cognition of reality.

Most Western scholars dismiss the notion of direct cognition because of its subjective nature. However. bv

1865.[6] The answer came to him in a dream as the image of a snake biting its tail. Upon waking, he immediately understood the image as a ring of carbon atoms. Along the same lines, Albert Einstein once said, "All great achievements of science must start from intuitive knowledge. At times I feel certain I am right while not knowing the reason."[7]

In his 1975 article published in *The Saturday Review*, Apollo 14 astronaut Edgar Mitchell gave a stunning example of direct cognition that occurred to him as he gazed on the Earth from lunar orbit:

> It began with the breathtaking experience
> of seeing planet Earth floating in the
> immensity of space—the incredible
> beauty of a splendid blue-and-white jewel
> floating in the vast, black sky. I
> underwent a religious-like peak

experience, in which the presence of
divinity became almost palpable and I
knew that life in the universe was not just
an accident based on random processes.
This knowledge, which came directly,
intuitively, was not a matter of discursive
reasoning or logical abstraction. It was
not deduced from information perceptible
by the sensory organs. The realization
was subjective, but it was knowledge
every bit as real and compelling as the
objective data the navigational program
or the communications system was based
on. Clearly, the universe has meaning and
direction—an unseen dimension behind
the visible creation that gives it an
intelligent design and gives life purpose.[8]

The reality that Plato describes does not exist outside
of us. It exists within consciousness and can be
discovered only through an introspective process.
Plato explains it as a realm of perfect forms, or ideas
that inform the mind and serve as the template for the
whole order of creation. These ideas are like rays of
spiritual light that shine into the human psyche from
higher realms of consciousness. We know them as the
ideals of goodness, truth, justice and beauty—what the

best and the brightest of every generation strive for above all else—or, as Plato puts it, "...what every soul

under careful examination, each one turns out to be inconsistent or only partially true. In the end, all glib answers are rejected, as if to say, "We cannot really know what justice is, only what it isn't."

Plato's method is reminiscent of the Zen master who gives the student a *koan* (riddle), for which there is no correct answer. Through this process, we come to learn that verbal answers keep us trapped in conceptual thinking and prevent the direct cognition of that which is non-conceptual, ever-present, and self-evident.

Plato's Impact on My Life

When the essential meaning of Plato's teaching fully dawned on me, it was as if I'd spent my whole life looking through the wrong end of a telescope until, suddenly, I was shown how to use it the right way. The result was a radical shift in my perspective, which I can best explain in terms of three insights. By insight, I mean the direct recognition of a self-evident truth.

The first insight is that the good, the true, the just, and the beautiful are not simply subjective notions that evolved through human consensus. They are realities or spiritual energies that shine into the human psyche from higher planes of consciousness. Almost everyone has an intuitive awareness (conscious or subconscious) of these energies. They function within us, individually and collectively, as our conscience, inner guidance, and sense of highest good. And it's this intuitive awareness that we tap into when we allow these ideals to guide us in our day-to-day lives.

The second insight is that right action follows from true knowledge and is always in our best interest. Once we realize that our highest ideals flow into the human psyche from higher dimensions of consciousness, it follows that it's in our self-interest to align with these ideals in whatever way we can. By doing so, we swim with the natural current of life instead of against it.

The third insight is that duality is an illusion. Although the world appears to be in a constant tug-of-war between opposites, there is only one motivating power in the universe. We can never define it or comprehend its essence. We can only know that it is Good in an

years, his unique method of inquiry has helped us grasp the most fundamental ideas in the human psyche—ideas that show us the truth of who we are and what we really want. To this day, these ideas remain deeply rooted in our language, our culture, and our most cherished institutions. Only a few individuals throughout history have made such a profound and sustaining impact on the evolution of civilization.

Endnotes – Chapter 3

[1] First century Roman copy of Greek original from the 4th century BC. Probably sculpted during Plato's lifetime. Capitoline Museum, Rome
https://www.britannica.com/biography/Plato/images-videos

[2] Wikipedia contributors, "Early life of Plato," *Wikipedia, The Free Encyclopedia,*
https://en.wikipedia.org/w/index.php?title=Early_life_of_Plato&oldid=812832168 (accessed May 14, 2018).

[3] Wikipedia contributors, "Early life of Plato."

[4] A.N. Whitehead, *Process and Reality (Gifford Lectures Delivered in the University of Edinburgh During the Session 1927-28)*, (Free Press, 1979), p. 39

[5] A. Bloom, *The Republic of Plato*, Book VII, 514a–520a (New York, NY; Basic Books, Second Edition; 1991). A futuristic adaptation of this story is depicted in the popular 1999 movie, *The Matrix*.

[6] Wikipedia contributors, "August Kekulé," *Wikipedia, The Free Encyclopedia*, https://en.wikipedia.org/w/index.php?title=August_Kekul%C3%A9&oldid=808249811 (accessed May 27, 2018).

[7] A. Calaprice, (Ed.), *The Expanded Quotable Einstein* (Princeton, NJ: Princeton University Press, 2000), p. 22, 287.

[8] E. Mitchell, "Outer Space to Inner Space: An Astronaut's Odyssey," *The Saturday Review*, February 22, 1975, p. 20-21

[9] A. Bloom, *The Republic of Plato*, Book VI, 505e (New York, NY: Basic Books, Second Edition, 1991).

Conscientious Objector

It's often said that periods of war and social upheaval bring out both the best and the worst in human nature. Perhaps it takes something violent and horrible to bring our highest ideals and deepest fears to the forefront. In this respect, the Vietnam War and the opposition that rose up in its wake are a case in point.

Before I recount my role in this opposition, I'd like to digress for a few pages and describe the social and political atmosphere during the early 1970s. For those who didn't live through this period, it's impossible to imagine how divided the country was—politically, socially, and spiritually.

The first US combat troops landed in Vietnam in March 1965. At the time, Vietnam was a small, impoverished nation that had been brutally exploited by French colonial occupation for almost a hundred years and by the Chinese for centuries before that. The conflict going on within its borders posed no threat to US interests.

The official reason for our involvement was that if Vietnam fell to communism, it would start a domino effect throughout Asia. In 1965, this theory resonated with the anticommunist hysteria of the 1950s that was still very much alive. As a result, President Lyndon Johnson and his administration enjoyed a modest level of public support during the early years of US involvement. But this early support was not to last. Unbeknownst to the politicians in Washington, a sea change was quietly sweeping across America.

By mid-1970, the US was entering its sixth year in a bloody campaign to stop the communist forces streaming down from North Vietnam. Things were not going well for our troops. During that year, more than 37,000 American soldiers were wounded or killed;[1] Vietnamese civilian and military casualties were often 10 to 15 times higher. The American public was completely unprepared for this level of carnage, not to mention the huge expenditure of resources that went with it. More and more, people began asking why we were engaged in what amounted to a civil conflict on the other side of the globe.

for pulling out in defeat. So every year, our generals and politicians doubled down with more troops and money, hoping for a breakthrough in a conflict we were clearly not winning. Meanwhile, the war grew increasingly unpopular as each planeload of body bags arrived home for burial.

After the Pentagon Papers[2] were leaked to the press in June 1971, a huge wave of opposition came crashing down on the politicians in Washington. These documents showed that the Johnson administration had been conducting a secret war in Cambodia and Laos and systematically lying about it to US Congress and the American public for years. The papers also showed that the war was not achieving its objectives and had little hope for success. These disclosures made it painfully obvious that the US was on the losing side of a civil war and that the North Vietnam regime was more resourceful and determined than our military had ever imagined possible. If our leaders had spent more time studying the history of the region and the character of the Vietnamese people, they would have reached this conclusion a decade earlier before inflicting so many casualties on both sides.

In addition to the obvious public aversion to bloodshed, there was another less visible reason for the shift in public opinion between 1965 and 1971. A profound change in consciousness had swept across North America, ushered in by the psychedelic experience and the spread of meditation and Eastern philosophy. A significant number of people now felt intuitively that we are all part of a greater whole. This sense of unity fostered a strong opposition to war in all forms.

Draft Resistance

In December 1969, the Selective Service began using a lottery system to create a pool of eligible young men for induction into the armed forces. The lottery drawing for those born during my birth year (1951) was conducted in a studio setting and broadcast over the radio in July 1970. I remember it was a warm afternoon and the broadcast could be heard from radios positioned in open windows all around campus.

Across the entire country, young men of my age
listened intently.

met. If the selection process reached number 127
before the end of the year, I would be drafted. If not,
then I'd be off the hook.

My prospects didn't look good. During the previous
year, the selection process had reached number 195.
While a student deferment would postpone my
induction until I finished college, I would most certainly
be drafted upon graduation in 1973. This situation
presented a moral dilemma—whether to participate in
an unjust war or to take steps to avoid the draft.

At the time, I didn't consider myself a pacifist. I would
have willingly joined the military to protect our
homeland from an enemy invasion. However, the idea
of killing or being killed because of an ideological
dispute with an impoverished people who posed no
threat to our country seemed absurd and
unconscionable. Most of the young men of my

generation felt the same way and wanted to avoid the draft by any means possible—legal or otherwise.

Dozens of methods were devised to avoid the draft, some of which were ingenious and amazingly effective. The most common approach was simply to disappear. Different sources estimate that 60,000 to 100,000 young men fled the country, mostly to Canada, Mexico, and Sweden.[3] Many of these expatriates still live abroad today even though they were officially pardoned by President Jimmy Carter in 1977.

At first blush, leaving the country sounded like a simple solution. But in fact, it was a drastic and possibly irreversible step. It meant leaving the past behind and creating a new life from scratch, essentially in exile. Moreover, if an expatriate ever wanted to return, he'd be facing a five-year federal prison sentence for draft evasion. As far as I was concerned, this option was not much better than simply getting drafted and taking my chances for the 18 months of required service.

The holy grail for draft resisters was the coveted 4-F classification, reserved for persons deemed unfit for military service. Essentially, this meant failing the Selective Service examination for physical and mental eligibility. For example, any men who were too short or too tall in relation to their weight would get a 4-F.

The exam also included psychological tests to weed out "mental defects," or homosexuals, which were classified as a "moral defects" by the Pentagon at that time. During the early years of the war, many men obtained a 4-F classification simply by pretending to be insane or homosexual. Depending on a young man's acting skills (or his sexual orientation), this method was initially fairly easy to pull off. However, as the war intensified, the examiners got wise to these practices and began to overlook bizarre behavior or admission of homosexuality even if a guy showed up wearing a dress, which many did.

Another common method to avoid induction was the age-old art of feigning illness. For example, men would take amphetamines and stay awake for days prior to the physical exam. If their heart rates and blood pressure were too high, they would be excused. But as the war progressed, the examiners became more adept at spotting malingerers and this method became less reliable.

My good friend, John Emory, devised an ingenious method. Upon receiving his induction notice, he went to a tattoo parlor and had the word "FUCK" tattooed in large bold letters along the outside edge of his right hand. The word was carefully placed so that when he saluted, the explicit message would be flashed at point-blank range. When he reported for his physical, the examiners took one look at his hand, shook their heads, and gave him a 4-F. Some years later after the war ended, he had the tattoo removed. Until then, he simply wore a bandage over it and only his close friends knew it was there.

Conscientious Objection

As much as I sympathized with anyone who faced being drafted, I just couldn't relate to any of these methods. I wasn't interested in simply avoiding the draft. I wanted to be excused legally, as a matter of conscience. And more importantly, I wanted to make an official statement of my opposition to the war.

The landmark 1965 Supreme Court ruling *United States v. Seeger* established that an individual did not

have to be a member of any organized religion or
recognized pacifist group in order to be a

from 1965 to 1970.[4] This meant that both public
opinion and the law had begun to shift in my favor.

Regardless of these changes, obtaining conscientious
objector status was by no means a slam-dunk. It
required navigating through several months of red tape,
culminating with a public hearing at my local draft
board. Even more disconcerting, it meant suffering the
disapproval and possible outrage of family and friends
who still supported the war in my small conservative
hometown.

Despite these obstacles, I went ahead and applied for
conscientious objector status in spring 1971. In
addition to an official application, I had to submit
affidavits from people in my community attesting to
my character and the sincerity of my beliefs. If my
application got past the initial hurdles, I would be

scheduled to appear before the local draft board to plead my case in person.

At the time, the conscientious objector status was divided into three sub-classifications. Sub-class 4-E applied to men who had a moral objection to service in any capacity. This classification was generally reserved for members of a strict pacifist religious community, such as the Quakers. Otherwise, the 4-E designation was almost impossible to get, even after the recent court rulings.

Sub-class 1-A-O applied to men who were morally opposed to carrying a weapon but willing to serve in the military in a noncombatant capacity. This sub-classification was the easiest to obtain, but not without a catch. The Army had a reputation for putting 1-A-Os into the medical corps, which was an extremely hazardous assignment. While I have great respect for any man who has served as a medic, the prospect of being in combat without a weapon did not appeal to me. And besides, this designation didn't address my basic opposition to the war on moral and philosophical grounds.

The third sub-class, 1-O, applied to men who were morally opposed to serving in the military but willing to do alternative nonmilitary service. This designation was difficult but not impossible to obtain and specific

had applied for exemption as a conscientious objector. In their eyes, I was committing a shameful act of selfishness and cowardice. Having gone through the depression and two world wars, they did not see the war in the same light as most of my generation. This confrontation brought my family relations to the breaking point. Emotions were high and I thought it very likely that my parents would disown me. I realized that the chances of success were low and that I might be creating huge rifts without producing any tangible results. Nevertheless, I decided to go forward and, if nothing else, to at least take a stand for common sense.

Two months after mailing my application, I was notified to appear for an interview at the local draft board in Lexington, Kentucky. When I showed up, the board members consisted of four men, three of whom I had known from childhood. They went over my application and asked several questions about my moral objection to war in general and to the Vietnam War in particular. Also, they wanted to know about my willingness to serve in a nonmilitary capacity. I remember that at one point, one of the men asked whether I considered myself a pacifist. I responded, "I don't know. All I know is that I don't want to kill anyone and I don't want to be killed." They seemed to accept that answer and shortly thereafter the interview ended. The board members were all very cordial but didn't give any hints about how their decision might go.

In August 1971, I received notification that my application had been approved and that my Selective Service classification had been officially changed to 1-O. I was stunned. I reread the letter a dozen times, wondering if I'd misread it or if there'd been a bureaucratic snafu. I felt vindicated and also gratified that the system did, in fact, have protections in place for people who opposed the war. Practically speaking, it turned out to be somewhat of a hollow victory. During 1971, the Selective Service called lottery numbers up to 125, just two numbers short of my number of 127.

The whole subject was dropped within my family and didn't come up again. But as the conflict dragged on, public opinion continued to shift strongly in opposition to the war. By the end of April 1973 when the last US

held convictions and respected me for it.

Several months after receiving my 1-O status, I reflected on all that had happened since I entered college in fall 1969. It seemed like a lifetime ago. The war and my response to it had impressed on me the importance of doing what I believed to be right and letting the chips fall where they may. I can't say that I've always had the foresight or the courage to put this lesson into practice, but in this instance at least, I had passed an important rite of passage.

Endnotes – Chapter 4

---

[1] Comptroller, Secy. of Defense, Vietnam Deaths and War Casualties by Month, http://www.americanwarlibrary.com/vietnam/vwc24.htm

[2] The Pentagon Papers were officially titled: *Report of the Office of the Secretary of Defense Vietnam Task Force.*

[3] Wikipedia contributors, "Draft evasion," *Wikipedia, The Free Encyclopedia,* https://en.wikipedia.org/w/index.php?title=Draft_evasion&oldid=913284264 (accessed September 13, 2019).

[4] "Conscientious Objectors" *Dictionary of American History, Encyclopedia.com.* http://www.encyclopedia.com/history/dictionaries-thesauruses-pictures-and-press-releases/conscientious-objectors

The Institute of Ability

By February 1971, I had begun a new stage in my journey—a life of yoga, meditation, and a strict vegetarian diet. I was on fire with enthusiasm and confident that I had found my rightful path. But I also sensed that I needed time to integrate these changes and consider my prospects for the future. I decided to take a semester off from college.

I didn't want to burn my bridges, so I made an appointment to see Dean Irby Cauthen and request a formal leave of absence. I remember going to his office just adjacent to the rotunda on the university lawn. Dean Cauthen was a gracious man who had a long and distinguished career at UVA. He was a gentleman in the best sense—a man loved and admired by students and faculty alike. Even though we had never spoken, he showed a genuine interest in my academic career, noting that I had made the Dean's List the previous three semesters. He agreed to my request and told me I'd be welcome to return anytime within the next 12 months. After that, I would have to reapply as a returning student. I thanked him and said that I planned to return in time for the fall semester that year.

I was living in Charlottesville at that time, with my friend and mentor Gibby Gibson. During the previous year, Gibby had attended a three-month yoga retreat in upstate New York with Dr. Ramamurti S. Mishra, author of *The Textbook of Yoga Psychology.*[1] Dr. Mishra was a medical doctor, a Sanskrit scholar, and a preeminent authority on the practice and philosophy of yoga.

Gibby suggested that we go to New York City and spend time with some of his friends who were also students of Dr. Mishra. I knew very little about yoga except what I had learned from Gibby, and Dr. Mishra's book was a complete enigma to me. Nonetheless, the possibility of hobnobbing with yoga students in New York was an adventure I didn't want to miss. I agreed enthusiastically. Within a few days, we were on the road to New York in my green 1970 Volkswagen.

When we arrived in New York, we found our way to the studio of Peter Max, an avid student of Swami

Manhattan in 1962. During the 1960's his "psychedelic art" became popular with the counterculture and frequently appeared on concert posters and magazine covers. In the early 1970s, his work was discovered by the mainstream media and became iconic in American pop culture.

Peter's studio was just as one might expect of an artist in the 1970s—a small cramped walkup flat with two rooms piled high with rolled posters, books, and magazines. The furniture consisted of an old sofa and a couple of drafting tables buried under various art projects. The walls were covered with Peter's art and several large photos of Swami Satchidananda. In the tiny kitchen, his fulltime macrobiotic chef was busy making lunch. I couldn't help but notice that the chef was a Hare Krishna devotee, complete with saffron robes, shaved head, and a *shikha* ponytail. The apartment and everything in it were a melting pot of spiritual ideas, artifacts, and icons from the East—all consumed, homogenized, and redefined by American New Age culture.

Shortly after we arrived, there came knock on the door and in walked Peter's friend Jeff Linzer. After making introductions, Jeff told us that he and three of his associates had recently opened the New York Center of the Institute of Ability. He also said they would be holding a three-day Enlightenment Intensive beginning the next day. Then he casually asked, "We have room for two more participants. Do you guys wanna come?" Without a moment's hesitation—or having the slightest idea of what an Enlightenment Intensive was—Gibby and I both said "Yes!" We looked at each other wide-eyed, hardly able to believe our good luck. We'd been in New York less than an hour and had already plugged into the exact kind of scene we had hoped to find.

We spent that night with some of Gibby's yoga buddies on Long Island, sleeping on the floor with a few cushions from the sofa. It was not a comfortable night, but we managed. One of the blessings of youth is the ability to get by in all kinds of situations. We had a sense of invincibility, or perhaps that some higher power was looking over us. We weren't always comfortable but were confident that our needs would be provided for.

way around the city. Before cell phones and map apps, finding an address meant driving around blindly and stopping frequently to ask directions. If you were lucky, you had a pencil and some notes scratched on the back of an envelope.

After some false leads, we eventually found the right building—an old brownstone in the west 70s just half a block from Central Park West. The Institute had rented the entire house to hold classes and serve as the offices and living quarters for Jeff Linzer and Stuart Friedman, the local instructors. Both had trained under Charles Berner, who founded the Institute in the mid-1960s.

Charles Berner

Charles Berner, later known as Sri Yogeshwar Muni, was an important teacher and developer of modalities in the field of personal development and conscious awakening.

Berner was born in 1927 and grew up in Southern California.[3] As a teenager, he gravitated toward spiritual interests and spent time visiting churches and spiritual communities in California. In the early 1950s, he became involved in the Church of Scientology, founded by L. Ron Hubbard. Scientology is a body of esoteric philosophies, some original and some borrowed from other traditions. It includes a psychotherapeutic practice called "auditing" that is designed to "clear" the mind and develop greater spiritual awareness. Berner rose in the organization and ultimately become president of the Church of Scientology in California.

After a falling out with L. Ron Hubbard, Berner left the church in 1966 and started teaching on his own. He flourished outside the confines of a large organization, attracting a sizeable number of dedicated students.

One morning in 1968, Berner had a profound awakening at the A&W Root Beer stand across the street from his office. While standing in line, watching people behind the counter, he realized in a flash that our state of mind is directly connected to our relationships and that the entire human condition revolves around this axis. In this realization, he saw his

received—releases us in some way from the bondage created by the mind. Over the next several months, he struggled to create a practical teaching that could help people break through their psychological conditioning and realize their own essential nature. What emerged was a group process called the Enlightenment Intensive, which became the foundation of his work. It consisted of a three-to-seven-day retreat using a basic format known as the Dyad Enlightenment Method, or the practice of self-inquiry in focused communication with a partner.[4]

Shortly after his realization, Berner founded The Institute of Ability and coined the term "Abilitism" to describe this new philosophy and approach to self-realization through inquiry and communication. He continued to develop and refine the Enlightenment Intensive through the mid-1970s.

Charles Berner, aka Sri Yogeshwar Muni (1927-2007)
Italy, circa 1997; courtesy of Karuna Laurel Hovde

In 1973, Berner met Sri Swami Kripalvananda (aka Swami Kripalu) while traveling in India. Swami Kripalu initiated him into Sahaja or Natural Yoga and gave him the name Sri Yogeshwar Muni. When Berner returned to the US, he started teaching Sahaja Yoga, renaming it Surrender Yoga and, later, Natural Meditation.

Over the years, his teaching shifted away from the Enlightenment Intensive in favor of Natural Meditation, which he considered to be a better approach to self-realization. In 1982, he moved to New South Wales, Australia, with a community of dedicated students.

There he continued to write and teach until his death in
2007

blankets and told to make a place for ourselves on the
floor where we'd sleep and keep our belongings. As
the other participants trickled in, we made
introductions, chatted, and joked about being
kidnapped by a nefarious cult.

The program started at 6:00 p.m. with a general
orientation and outline of the program. Since 10 of us
would be living together for three days in close
quarters, certain ground rules had to be observed.
There were strict protocols regarding interaction with
other participants and the instructors. There was one
bathroom and we'd get one break per hour. Meals
would be light and sleeping would be on the floor,
limited to six hours per night.

In case it wasn't obvious when we arrived, it was now
crystal clear that we were in for three days of austerity.
I was a bit apprehensive but also excited about the

prospect. I think everyone in the group felt the same way. We were all young and eager to experience what Abilitism had to offer.

After the orientation, we were given specific instructions about the Dyad Enlightenment Method, which would be our primary activity for the next three days. The method is essentially a form of self-inquiry focused on the question, "Who am I?" We'd be working in pairs and addressing the question in a specific way. One person would begin the process as the interrogator by saying, "Tell me who you are." At that point, the interrogators role is to listen, be attentive, and maintain eye contact. The respondent's first job is focused introspection on the question—not simply repeating it mindlessly but looking within to locate the "I" or "me." The respondent's second and equally important job is to communicate whatever thoughts or insights come up, regardless of how vague or nonsensical they may seem. After five minutes, a bell rings and the roles are reversed.

After the introduction, we had a light supper consisting of salad with raw tahini and a few roasted nuts. It was sparse—barely enough to make a dent in my appetite. But I had fasted before and wasn't too concerned about the meager rations. I figured that I could handle anything for three days. We were instructed not to talk during meals, but rather to focus on our question. All

another. The bell rang and each interrogator said to their partner, "Tell me who you are." For five minutes, the room was silent except for the quiet murmurs of people trying to answer their question. Then the bell rang again and we switched roles. This went on for 45 minutes, followed by a 15-minute break. During the break, we could use the bathroom and do some light exercise or stretching. Then we began again with new partners. This hour-long process comprised one round. We did four rounds that evening. Little did I know that we'd be doing 14 rounds the next day.

Around midnight, we stopped and prepared for "sleep meditation". We were allowed to lie down but were supposed to keep our question in the back of our minds. I remember lying down with my blanket and trying to focus on my question. But I was too exhausted and quickly fell asleep—at least for a while. Sleeping on the floor is never comfortable and no one slept very well. And to make sure we didn't sleep too much, an instructor would walk through the room periodically during the night, saying, "Let your body sleep, but you stay with your question."

We were awakened at 6:00 a.m. and told to get ready to resume the Dyad process. Just getting everyone through the morning ablutions with only one tiny bathroom took almost an hour. Then we had breakfast consisting of a small bowl of hot cereal and herbal tea. Like Oliver Twist, I was tempted to ask, "Please, sir, may I have some more?" But I didn't dare. In any event, I'm sure the answer would have been "No." We were deliberately kept on austerity rations, which I assumed had evolved that way for a reason.

By 8:00 a.m., we were all seated on cushions and ready to begin; question, followed by five minutes of mumbling, followed by the bell; question, mumbling, bell—again and again and again. One might think that the interrogator's role was easy. But in fact, both roles were difficult. The respondent's role required focused attention on what was really there inside—or what wasn't there, as the case might be. Yet in some ways, the interrogator's role was even more difficult. It was challenging to stay attentive and listen to the nonsense coming out of the other person. And with almost no sleep the night before, the task became a contest merely to keep the eyelids open. To address this

rounds and breaks became a blur. Eventually I lost track of time and the number of rounds we'd done. It didn't seem to matter. As the day ground on, I completely ran out of things to say. My responses became five minutes of "uuuuh" followed by long spans of silence. I had taken inventory of the same warehouse of memories and impressions a hundred times. It included my name, body, background, education, likes and dislikes, aches and pains, fears and desires. It was an impressive list of descriptions, attributes, and character traits covering every nook and cranny of my life. But somehow, it all missed the point. My mind was just treading water in a pool of thoughts that were getting increasingly stale with each passing round. I kept asking myself, "Who is the one behind all these thoughts?" The more I tried to grab hold of that one, the more he eluded me.

The second day ended around midnight. Finally, I could close my eyes and have a respite. I slept deeply, despite the hard floor and the occasional murmurs of a roaming instructor, "Let your body sleep, but you stay with your question."

The third day started at 6:00 a.m. and with a little less enthusiasm than the day before. I wondered if anything good was happening, but I wasn't hopeful. All I could think of was a nice meal, an unrushed shower, and a soft bed. I wondered if anyone else in the group was so shallow and materialistic, and so ready to get out of there. We had a long day ahead of us, so I stopped whining to myself, put on my game face, and stepped into the day.

At some point after lunch, I thought, "What the hell." A burst of fresh energy rose up urging me to give 100 percent. I started looking within myself with total concentration and determination to find out who or what was behind all my thoughts and experiences— that thing I called "me." In one last push, I tried to get behind myself.

The situation was like the drunk searching on his hands and knees under a streetlight. A policeman walks by and asks, "What are you doing?" The drunk

says, "I'm looking for my keys." The policeman tries to
 ̄ ̇ ̇‚‚ and then asks, "Are you sure

I was looking for myself in my ‚‚‚‚
became obvious that I couldn't possibly be in my mind.
Yet like the drunk in the story, the only place I could
look was in my mind. To borrow from U.G.
Krishnamurti, I realized simultaneously two equal and
opposing facts: (1) The mind is the only instrument I
have to inquire who I am, and (2) it's the *wrong*
instrument.[5] The juxtaposition of these two facts
caused a short circuit. My mind came to a full stop. In
that instant, there was an almost visible flash inside
my head accompanied by a popping sound. I felt
myself freefalling in an unbounded spaciousness that
was everywhere and nowhere. The clarity of the
moment rippled through me and filled all my yearnings
for wholeness and connection.

The question was unanswerable. I started to laugh at
the absurdity of my efforts. I laughed and laughed and
couldn't stop. I put my hand over my mouth but it was
no use. Huge guffaws shook the room. At first the

other participants just stopped and stared. Then it caught on and everyone joined in. The instructors tried to restore order but it was hopeless. The whole room filled with gales of laughter. As if on cue, I was scooped up and escorted out of the room.

We'd been told that if we had a breakthrough, we should raise our hand and request an interview with the senior instructor. I don't remember if I raised my hand, but I was ushered upstairs and down a long hallway. I entered a room that was empty except for two tall gothic chairs facing each other. Jeff Linzer was sitting in one of the chairs and motioned for me to sit opposite.

When I sat down, he simply looked at me and said, "So, tell me who you are." I don't remember exactly what I said. I was so full of energy and laughter that I'm sure my response was nonsense. Jeff just nodded and was quiet for a moment. Then he asked very casually, "So tell me, Bart, how old are you?"

The question shocked me and opened a whole new dimension of my realization. I saw immediately that it was a trick question. Without hesitating, I said, "I'm not any age at all. I haven't even been born yet!" Then Jeff asked the first question in a slightly different way.

“So, what are you then?” I replied, “I am pure

... looked down and said. “That’s

...

of my realization. In any event, ...
had genuinely realized who I am. But even if he had doubted, it wouldn’t have mattered to me in the least. The genie was out of the bottle and riding a wave of unchecked energy.

Jeff cautioned me to be as quiet as possible and hold the new energy inside. He said that for my sake and for the others, it was important for me to return to the group, continue the process, and not discuss what had happened. Instinctively, I knew he was right. I took a few minutes to settle myself and went back downstairs to join the group.

Whatever had happened to me began happening to others. People were going off like popcorn. By the end of the day, more than half the participants experienced some kind of *satori*—a clear, sudden, and direct experience of one’s pure essential nature beyond the body-mind-personality complex.

In many ways, this experience was not new to me. I
had experienced it while on LSD and also during
meditation. However, three features of this new
experience made it unique and more powerful. First, it
was not a momentary flash but a sustained experience
that extended through time. Second, it placed me
simultaneously in time and outside of it—both within
and beyond the boundaries of the relative world. Third,
the experience was outside of any meditative or drug-
induced state, with eyes open and the mind fully
engaged in activity.

Immediately I remembered Maharishi's description of
the fourth state of consciousness, in which the
unbounded nature of consciousness is maintained
while the mind is fully engaged in activity. This left me
with no doubt that I was experiencing what Maharishi
called Cosmic Consciousness. It was as if for the first
time I was free from the confines of the body and mind
and had returned to my true self. When I gazed at
another person or even a bird sitting on a branch, I felt
as if I were looking into a mirror. I could see myself
staring back at me.

The Enlightenment Intensive ended around eight that
evening. Eight of the 10 participants had profound
enlightenment experiences. Neither before nor since

have I encountered a process that produced such

~~'' :~ ~~~h a short~~ period of time. I give

~~Gibby and Pop~~

Manhattan. All that evening I was on fire. The experience of my unbounded nature never diminished or wavered, even during sleep. To call it an experience implies a subject-object duality that didn't exist. I simply was myself—an unlimited, unlocatable, and unknowable presence—looking through the body-mind instrument as one might look through a telescope.

By late afternoon of the next day, something started to happen. My expanded state of awareness began to contract, and the body-mind, with all its neuroses and hang-ups, started to reassert itself. It was horrifying, like being squeezed into a corpse. At first, I was in denial and refused to believe it. I thought, "How could this happen? How can I lose the truth of what I am? Maybe I just need to close my eyes and get centered." But that didn't help and by evening it was clear that I had lost it and there was nothing I could do to get it back—whatever "it" was.

This was the most devastating loss of my life up to that time. Looking back, I can see that it affected me even more deeply than I realized at the time. It was years later when I finally gained some insight and clarity about what had happened.

One essential feature of higher states of consciousness is the ability of the nervous system to function on multiple levels simultaneously. In ordinary circumstances, this kind of multilevel functioning is rare. The closest example is what musicians and athletes describe as playing in "the zone"— performances that require total concentration and complete abandonment at the same time. This requires a highly developed nervous system.

During the Enlightenment Intensive, the extreme one-pointed focus apparently launched me into a higher state of consciousness. Unfortunately my nervous system couldn't maintain it for more than a few days. After experiencing dozens of similar episodes over the years, it's become clear that attaining a higher state of consciousness is not all that difficult. Sustaining it is another thing altogether. As much as I admire Charles Berner and his brilliant work, the Enlightenment Intensive offered only a glimpse into higher states of consciousness. The work required to transform the

nervous system so that it can maintain these higher
· ··· ···ars or possibly lifetimes.

Intensive. From what I've read of
Swami Kripalu, this style of meditation bears a strong
resemblance to TM—the very spiritual practice I began
with in 1970.

Endnotes – Chapter 5

[1] R. S. Mishra, M.D., *The Textbook of Yoga Psychology–A New Translation and Interpretation of Patanjali's Yoga Sutras* (The Julian Press, 1963).

[2] Wikipedia contributors, "Peter Max," *Wikipedia, The Free Encyclopedia,* https://en.wikipedia.org/w/index.php?title=Peter_Max&oldid= 831504466 (accessed July 18, 2018).

[3] C. Berner; Y. Wexler (Ed.), *Enlightenment and the Enlightenment Intensive: Volumes 1 and 2* (Independent Publishing, 1973).

[4] Wikipedia contributors, "Enlightenment Intensive," *Wikipedia, The Free Encyclopedia,*

https://en.wikipedia.org/w/index.php?title=Enlightenment_Inte
nsive&oldid=806764248 (accessed Aug. 23, 2018).

[5] U. G. Krishnamurti, *No Way Out: Conversations with U.G.
Krishnamurti* (Smriti Books, 2005), Ch. 6.

Dark Night of the Soul

From 1969 to 1976, I skated through life as carefree student. Everything I needed and more seemed to land in my lap. My studies were not particularly challenging and I had plenty of time to pursue my passions— meditation, philosophy, and the esoteric teachings of India and Tibet. When I wasn't attending classes, I was reading, talking or thinking about these topics in one form or another.

After I graduated from UVA, my grandmother gave me $2,000. It seemed like a fortune at the time. This allowed me to spend the next two years in Europe, attending long meditation retreats with other spiritual seekers from around the world. These were the most blissful years of my life.

When I returned from Europe in spring 1976, I was broke and without any direction. The bliss of student life was over and the harsh reality of adulthood landed on me with full force. I had no idea where to go or how I was going to support myself.

Premonitions

The one bright spot in my life was Anne Huggins. Our relationship is an important part of this story, not only because of how it began but also because of the role she has played in my life and development ever since.

I first met Anne in September 1973 in the village of Lenzerheide, Switzerland, about 25 miles south of Chur near the Austrian border. We

Anne Huggins,
Lenzerheide, Switzerland, 1973

were both attending a training course to become TM teachers. I had a strong intuition that we were going to be married as soon as I met her. I've had this kind of

premonition frequently throughout my life. It's a
~~knowing~~ or seeing something as a fact, without the

~~Anne was very ...~~
were going to be married and that was that.

After we chatted for a few minutes, I told her about my
premonition. That was not a wise move. She made it
clear that she was not looking for a relationship and
had no interest in me. Despite this awkward beginning,
we soon became friends and I learned to keep my
premonitions to myself.

During the next few years, Anne warmed up to me and
we developed a close bond. We eventually married in
Woodside, California, and have been together 46 years.
I have no doubt that she is the best possible partner for
me and, more importantly, that our meeting and
subsequent marriage were part of my spiritual destiny.

I've had various kinds of premonitions throughout my
life. They started as early as I can remember, and I
quickly learned when I should pay close attention.

Often these perceptions are mundane and insignificant—like having a thought of someone just before they call or knowing that a certain letter will arrive in the mail that day.

However, occasionally I have a different kind of intuitive experience—a strong, almost overpowering, sense of destiny. It's as if I'm standing at a crossroads and can clearly see that one road is in alignment with my future. These kinds of premonitions don't happen very often. But when they do, they are invariably correct and have guided me through some of the most important decisions of my life. The first time this happened was when I saw the picture of Maharishi in 1968 and knew that I would learn a meditation practice. The second time was when I met Anne and immediately knew that we would be married.

I had a similar premonition in 1980 when I first heard about the reinsurance business. Without really knowing anything about reinsurance, I had a strong sense that this would be my future career. Within a few months, we moved across the country and I began a new job with a reinsurance firm in Seattle. This turned out to be an exceptional opportunity in a budding industry that was on the brink of exponential growth. The work was high pressure and all consuming, but the monetary compensation was exceptional. By the time I left the reinsurance business in 1996, we were

The term "Dark Night of the Soul" comes from a poem by the 16th century Spanish mystic St. John of the Cross. Although the poem was left untitled, the author used the metaphor of a dark night to describe the soul's journey in search of the Divine. The term has since been commonly used to describe a spiritual crisis or when a person feels abandoned, bereft, and without direction. This pretty much sums up my situation from 1980 to 1985.

I have always been a sensitive person—perhaps more vulnerable than most to the slings and arrows of adult life. This trait, combined with the pressures of a new job, a mortgage, and a young marriage, made me particularly susceptible to imbalance during this period. To make things worse, I was working long hours, eating poorly, and not getting enough exercise or rest. As I spiraled out of control, I failed to see the obvious warning signs. I tried to sit for daily meditation, but my mind was a treadmill of stressful and anxious thoughts. I was unhappy, depressed, and feeling disconnected from the experience of unity that had nurtured me through the previous decade.

I think a significant part of my unhappiness was due to my own difficulty in growing up. By that I mean taking responsibility for my choices and not depending on others for support. Growing up is not something that happens at any prescribed time in life. It's a psychological shift that can occur at any age, or not at all. But young or old, growing up is never easy and I think this is particularly true for men. The little boy in us rebels against it.

During spring 1983, my mental and emotional condition grew tenuous. I fell into a deep depression and started having full-blown panic attacks. I looked relatively normal on the surface. But underneath, I was a wreck. My work involved a brutal schedule of travel, making presentations, negotiating contracts, and supervising a small staff. All the while, I felt like I was on the brink of insanity. I wondered if my condition stemmed from past drug use. Perhaps the residual effects of 60 LSD trips were finally catching up with me. But in truth, I had no idea why I was falling apart or if I would ever regain my equilibrium. This uncertainty made the situation even more terrifying.

know how I would have gotten through this period without her. At night as I lay in bed, I held onto her like a shipwrecked sailor clinging to a buoy. My body trembled. In the morning, the sheets had a strange odor. I finally had to face the fact that I was having some kind of emotional breakdown. The prospect that I might have to resign from my job loomed over me like a dark cloud.

Wrathful Deities

Looking back, I believe this experience was a manifestation of my shadow side coming to the forefront. Sigmund Freud and, later, Carl Jung used the term "shadow" to describe hidden parts of our psyche that assert their influence though unconscious behavior or dreams. In its essence, the shadow represents painful (and unclaimed) impressions and feelings from our past—psychic wounds of shame, guilt, fear, and rage that we've spent a lifetime trying to avoid.[1]

Because of the negative emotions associated with the shadow, we tend to think of it as something to be avoided or gotten rid of altogether. On the contrary, Jung emphasized the importance of working with the shadow and discovering what it can teach us. He considered the shadow to be a potential ally and the doorway to our individuality.[2] One way or another, we must face these demons and allow them to take their rightful place at the table, along with the nobler angels of our nature. For better or worse, these opposing aspects of the personality make up the tangled paradox of being human.

In his groundbreaking work *Integral Spirituality*, Ken Wilber describes four branches of human development—waking up, growing up, cleaning up, and showing up.[3] Cleaning up—the process of facing and working with one's shadow material—is an essential step, particularly for the spiritual aspirant. In the process of discovering higher dimensions of reality, the shadow side invariably comes to the surface demanding to be seen and heard. The more we try to push it away, the stronger it asserts itself into our thoughts and behavior, either consciously or unconsciously.

decade since I had read this book, the teaching about wrathful deities flashed in my mind in connection with my present crisis. I found the book in my bookcase and reread the chapters pertaining to these dark energies that arise from the subconscious regions after death.

The teachings advise the listener to relax, let go, and meet the wrathful deities without resistance. Because they are reflections of our own inner fear and aggression, any resistance is like throwing fuel on a fire. The ancient sages tell us to meet these energies with compassion and gratitude—compassion because they represent the wounded parts of ourselves crying out to be healed and gratitude because they can teach us who we are in the fullest sense, as multidimensional beings. What a godsend this book was for me at a time when I most needed it!

For me, facing the shadow was like standing on the edge of a dark abyss. It took all my strength to avoid being sucked in. I had no idea what was down there but I sensed it was horrible and inescapable. In comparison, my experience with LSD seemed like a child's game. Now the stakes were higher. I realized that I had to let go and allow myself to fall into the abyss, trusting that I would come out somewhere on the other side. The only way out was in.

Grace from Higher Dimensions

During my life, I've gotten into a number of scrapes of one kind or another. Most were brought on by my own hubris—the near lethal combination of youth and testosterone. Others were less avoidable. And yet no matter how difficult the situation, I've always found that help was available when I asked for it. This crisis was no exception.

As I lay in bed one night, I silently prayed that this curse be removed from me. I fell asleep exhausted with this petition still on my lips. Sometime in the night, I awoke. At first, I felt myself lying in bed and everything seemed familiar. But then I was unable to move my limbs and realized that I was dreaming. Today, this experience is called lucid dreaming. It has happened to me periodically ever since I was a child. Although I didn't know the terminology, I was

distress of my situation had vanished. When I looked down, I could clearly see my body lying in bed next to Anne. Then I began to move through the ceiling as if being pulled by an invisible force. I could feel the texture of the sheetrock and wood as I passed through. At the same time, I heard loud, almost painful, noises like the grinding of gears. Then I popped out on the other side and continued to ascend. I felt a sense of relief to be floating freely again.

Then I came up against another barrier without knowing what it was. The process repeated itself. I was pushed through with the same accompanying noise and a feeling of relief when I came out the other side. I continued to ascend in this way, passing through several more barriers until finally I came to a stop. I didn't know where I was, but there was something familiar about the extraordinary colors and textures around me. From my past ventures with LSD, I recognized this experience of hyper-reality, or what is sometimes called enhanced consciousness.

Hyper-reality is not something easily explained to someone who's never had the experience. It's like stepping out of a dimly lit room into the full light of day. The visual images are sharper, the colors more brilliant, and the textures more complex. The ordinary waking state seems dull and out of focus by comparison. In fact, the hallmark of this experience is that everything appears more solid and more real than the so-called "real world" of the waking state.

Hyper-reality is one of a dozen or so commonly reported features of the near-death experience. (See Chapter 7.) Dutch cardiologist, Pim van Lommel, coined the term "enhanced consciousness" to describe this experience. During his 20 years of research at Rijnstate Hospital in The Netherlands, Dr. Lommel has documented hundreds of cases of enhanced consciousness during episodes of cardiac arrest, when all respiration and brainwave activity has ceased. Out of several hundred patients who were successfully resuscitated, about 18 percent reported the experience of enhanced consciousness often accompanied by a near-death experience. Dr. Lommel's findings have been published in *The Lancet* [5] and in his book *Consciousness Beyond Life.*[6]

but it was empty like a pool of clear light. As bizarre as this sounds, his presence felt familiar and the lack of clear features didn't seem unusual. I believe I was experiencing my higher dimensional self. Each of us has a higher self, sometimes called a "guide" or "guardian angel" that accompanies us through life. Its role is that of intermediary between our human self and our soul, helping us become a more authentic expression of our soul during our earth experience.

No words were spoken and yet we communicated telepathically with ease and clarity. I could hear his thoughts and knew that he could hear mine. Communicating this way seemed natural and reinforced a certain intimacy between us. From my elevated perspective, I could see that we are all linked together in the field of consciousness, even though this linkage is not apparent here on the earth plane.

He opened the book and held it out for me to read. It contained my entire life—past, present, and future. The events recorded in the book may seem trivial to anyone else. Yet each entry bore a special significance to me—either a difficult challenge or a period of my life when I had succeeded or fallen short in some way. I could see that my life is a joint project between my human self and my soul. My role in this project is to listen deeply and to give clear expression to my soul nature through my speech and actions. I was glad to see the times when I had succeeded in doing this. Yet there was never a sense of failure when I fell short. I could see that I had all the time in the world to keep practicing.

A thousand images whirled through my mind as I scanned the pages. As each image fell into place, I better understood the nature of the soul and the purpose of human life. Our earth lives are just a tiny part of a much bigger picture. And these physical bodies are only temporary vehicles that we use to interact with the physical world. The whole point of human life is to experience limitations and challenges that otherwise we'd have no way to know.

It was at this point that my guide drew attention to an entry in the book—the spiritual crisis I was suffering at

the time. The irony of the situation immediately
flashed in my mind. I had gone to bed asking for this

quantum leap in my spiritual growth, one that
otherwise could take lifetimes to accomplish.

Reentry into the Physical World

When I awoke the next morning, nothing had changed.
And yet everything was different. I was still having
panic attacks and my physical and emotional
condition was tenuous. But I saw my situation in a
completely new light. The dark abyss of dread now
seemed impersonal and less ominous. It was simply
fear without an object, made threatening only by the
energy required to keep it suppressed. The sensation
of fear was still arising in me, but as strange as it
sounds, I was no longer afraid of it. I trusted that the
process was a gift, just as my spirit guide had shown
me. I felt like Ebenezer Scrooge on Christmas morning.
Everything was the same as before, but my attitude
had changed. And that made all the difference.

During the next six months, I learned to work with the fear as it arose—not by pushing it away or distracting myself but by facing it and letting go of any resistance. I had to accept the fact that, after all, this dark material was a product of my own thoughts and behavior. Gradually, I learned how to meet the waves of fear and allow them to pass through me. As I became more skilled in this process, the intensity abated. I began to feel more grounded and to enjoy little things again. But more importantly, I was hopeful and positive about the future.

For several years afterward, I made the conscious decision not to discuss the experience with anyone except Anne. For one thing, I just didn't have the words to describe what had happened. For another, I thought most people would probably think I was delusional. In my own mind, I knew that I had received a genuine communication from higher dimensions of consciousness—a response to the crisis that was at hand. Even though the communication was symbolic in nature, it struck home with clarity and impressed on me that we all have access to support and guidance from higher places within ourselves.

One day while having lunch with some friends, the subject of out-of-body experiences came up. Without even thinking, I let it slip that I'd had one. Everyone at the table became quiet. Somewhat timidly, I began

Looking back at this episode 35 years later, I see it as the most difficult and painful period of my life. Yet if I had the power to go back, I wouldn't change a single detail. I was deeply humbled by the fragility of my mental and emotional constitution. The sense of invincibility that I carried as a youth was gone. But I had gained optimism and confidence in the spiritual resources that are available when we most need them.

Ernest Hemingway once wrote, "The world breaks everyone and afterward many are strong at the broken places." [7]

Endnotes – Chapter 6

[1] "Carl Jung and the Shadow: The Hidden Power of Our Dark Side"; *Academy of Ideas*, December 2015; https://academyofideas.com/2015/12/carl-jung-and-the-shadow-the-hidden-power-of-our-dark-side/

[2] "Carl Jung and the Shadow: The Hidden Power of Our Dark Side"; *Academy of Ideas*, December 2015.

[3] K. Wilber, *Integral Spirituality: A Startling New Role for Religion in the Modern and Postmodern World* (Boulder, CO: Shambhala Publications, 2007).

[4] W. Y. Evans-Wentz (Ed.), *The Tibetan Book of the Dead; or The After-Death Experiences on the Bardo Plane* (Oxford University Press, 1967, 4th Edition, 2000).

[5] P. van Lommel, R. van Wees, V. Meyers, and I. Elfferich; "Near-death Experience in Survivors of Cardiac Arrest: A prospective study in the Netherlands," *The Lancet*, Volume 358, no. 9298, 2039-2045

[6] P. van Lommel, *Consciousness Beyond Life* (HarperOne, 2011).

[7] E. Hemingway, *A Farewell to Arms* (Scribner, 1995), Ch. 34

Death and the Afterlife

Death became a major theme in my life at an early age. When I was seven years old, my grandfather died suddenly from a heart attack while tending his garden. My grandmother found him slumped against the garden shed with the watering hose still in his hand. Naturally, the family was shocked and grief-stricken. But for me, the event triggered a deeper and more existential crisis. For the first time I was confronted with the reality of death—that a person is alive one moment and gone the next. And that someday this would happen to me.

My worldview was turned upside down overnight. Suddenly, life seemed hard and non-negotiable. I questioned the point of living if eventually we're all going to die. For weeks, I was distraught and could hardly eat. Everyone assumed I was grieving the loss of my grandfather. But compared to this shocking revelation about death, my grandfather's passing seemed unimportant. What does it matter if one man dies when the whole world is going to die?

At one point, my mother saw me crying and tried to comfort me. "What's the matter?" she asked. "I'm going to die," I said, sobbing. She tried to comfort me. "Don't worry. You're not going to die for a long time." This response did nothing to console me. The fact that death was a future event didn't mitigate the problem at all. Sooner or later, I would have to face death by myself. And neither my mother nor any of the adults in the world could do anything about it. From that point on, I had a burning desire to know what happens after we die. Are we simply gone? Lights out? Or is there an afterlife? These were urgent questions for me.

During the next few years, I would sometimes ask adults who I thought might know the answer—relatives, teachers, or the minister at church. Their responses were always disappointing. No one seemed to know the answer, which only compounded my problem. I wondered, "How is this possible? We're all going to die, yet no one seems concerned about it. Isn't anyone afraid or at least curious?" Eventually, the urgency of the question subsided. It was apparent that no one had the answer or even wanted to talk about it.

Republic, he narrates the story of Er—the first written account of a near-death experience.[1] As the story unfolds, a Greek soldier named Er is wounded in combat and left for dead on the battlefield. Several days later when his relatives come to retrieve the body, he is revived and gives a detailed account of his experiences in the afterlife. These passages were like nourishment to my soul. They assured me that I wasn't alone in sensing the importance of these questions.

The Near-Death Experience

Sometime around 1985, I came across *Life After Life* by Dr. Raymond Moody.[2] This book marked a turning point for me in my quest to learn more about death and to understand my out-of-body experience, which had occurred in 1983. (See Chapter 6.)

Dr. Moody received a PhD in philosophy from the University of Virginia (UVA) in 1969, the same year I arrived as a freshman. He went on to earn another PhD in psychology from the University of West Georgia and, later, an MD from the Medical College of Georgia. In 1976, he returned to UVA where he completed his residency in psychiatry. Although I didn't know Dr. Moody during my time at UVA, I met him some 30 years later and was delighted to discover how much we had in common. We both attended UVA, majored in philosophy, studied under many of the same professors, and shared a deep appreciation for Plato. More importantly, we both shared a lifelong interest in the subject of death and the afterlife.

During his undergraduate studies at UVA, Moody had the good fortune to meet Dr. George Ritchie, clinical professor of psychiatry in the School of Medicine. From the outset, Moody was impressed by Dr. Ritchie's clinical experience and professionalism. It came as somewhat of a shock to learn that as a young man, Dr. Ritchie had experienced the "afterlife" during an episode of cardiac arrest. Moody decided to attend a talk given by Dr. Ritchie about this experience.

In winter 1943, Ritchie was a 20-year-old private in the US Army, at Camp Barkeley, Texas. After contracting pneumonia, he was placed in critical care at the camp hospital. As his condition worsened, he lapsed into a

see everything that was going on, including the resuscitation attempts and preparation of his body for the morgue. Eventually, a "being of light" arrived and took him into another dimension where he was shown different realms in the afterlife. Finally, the spirit guide told him that he would have to return to his physical body. Ritchie's first reaction was to protest, but before he could say anything, he felt himself being pushed back into his body.

About this same time, a hospital attendant noticed a slight movement in the sheet over Ritchie's face and immediately called for help. A doctor rushed in and quickly injected adrenaline into Ritchie's heart. This was a Hail Mary procedure in those days, but his heart began beating again after a lapse of more than nine minutes. The full account of Dr. Ritchie's experience is detailed in his book *Return from Tomorrow*.[3]

While listening to Dr. Ritchie's story, Moody remembered the story of Er, in Plato's *Republic*. Like many scholars, Moody assumed that Plato had used this story as an allegorical device, not to be taken literally. But now he was hearing a firsthand account of a similar experience from a highly respected professor and medical doctor. Although he tried to be open-minded, the story just didn't fit into his Western scientific perspective. He filed it in the back of his mind as a fascinating but singular event.

Several years later, Moody was teaching philosophy at East Carolina University. One day after class, a student came to his office and shared his own afterlife experience, which had occurred years earlier after an automobile accident. Moody was dumfounded. He'd now heard two firsthand accounts of a lucid experience during cardiac arrest—something considered impossible from a Western medical perspective. He was forced to consider whether these were freak events or examples of a recurring phenomenon. If the latter, why hadn't he read about this phenomenon during his years of study in medicine and psychology?

The next day, he revised his curriculum to include discussion of these afterlife experiences. Eventually, he earned the nickname "professor death," which attracted the interest of other students and faculty who wanted to share their own stories. When an article

convinced that the stories represented a genuine and recurring phenomenon.[4]

The next year, Moody enrolled in medical school where he had the opportunity to interview hospital patients who had survived cardiac arrest and were documented to be "clinically dead" during the time of their experience. He later coined the term "near-death experience" (NDE) to describe this phenomenon and eventually collected over 1,000 accounts, many of which were published in his bestselling books *Life After Life* (1975) and *The Light Beyond* (1988).

Science and the Near-Death Experience

After Moody's first book was published, several researchers studied the NDE phenomenon and confirmed his findings. For example, Dr. Pim van Lommel, a cardiologist from The Netherlands, found that roughly 18 percent of patients who were resuscitated after cardiac arrest were able to recall some elements of an NDE.[5]

In a 1992 Gallup poll, 13 million people in the US—roughly five percent of the population at the time—reported having had an NDE at some point in their lives. Despite its prevalence many people tend to dismiss the experience as a dream, hallucination, or delusion triggered by oxygen deprivation. These explanations persist even though they've been disproven repeatedly.

The age-old assumption is that consciousness is produced by the brain and therefore cannot possibly survive death of the body. However, a growing number of scientists are challenging this assumption with a new theory—that consciousness is a fundamental property of the universe like gravity or electromagnetism. As such, it exists independently. The brain merely acts as an interface, coordinating the exchange of energy and information between the nonlocal field of consciousness and the physical world.[6] This view of consciousness as a basic property of the universe is not new. In 1931, the physicist and Nobel laureate Max Planck said the following:

I regard consciousness as fundamental. I regard matter as derivative from consciousness. We

BCE. In this text, the Sanskrit word *sat* refers to both existence and consciousness, indicating that the ancient sages considered these ideas to be different aspects of the same reality.[8]

Becoming a Hospice Volunteer

It's impossible to delve into the subject of death without acknowledging the immense suffering in modern society around this issue. Grief and bereavement are natural reactions after the death of a loved one. But unfortunately, there's a deeper and more harmful reaction to death that infects modern society—one that prevents people from accepting and appreciating the natural cycles of life.

The very mention of death is often considered impolite or even taboo, particularly when someone is gravely ill. It's as if death were unnatural or a failure on the part of modern medicine. And although no one ever says so, there's an underlying sense that even those who are dying have failed in some way—failed to take proper care of their bodies, failed to overcome their disease, or simply failed in living.

Most people live in denial as if death will never come. Consider the customary procedure after someone dies. The body is immediately covered with a sheet and whisked away—a practice that has evolved solely to hide the grim reality of a dead body. But who are we really trying to protect, and from what?

Even more bizarre are the efforts people make to postpone death or circumvent it altogether. In the US alone, billions of dollars are spent on supplements that promise to extend human life to 120 years or longer. And if life extension isn't enough, there's a growing industry in cryonics. For a mere $200,000, your body can be frozen and stored in liquid nitrogen in the hope that science will someday make it possible to revive it. The fact that no one in mainstream science believes this will ever be possible doesn't stop people from signing up. As of this writing, more than 250 people in the US have been cryopreserved and more than 1,500 have paid to have the procedure performed upon their death.[9]

Our behavior around death is riddled with these kinds of contradictions, all of which betray a deep psychosis

matter how small, to promote a more sane and compassionate approach and to raise our collective consciousness around death. When I first learned about the Hospice organization and their work to support the dying and their families, I was immediately drawn to their vision.

I completed the hospice training in 1999 and began working as a volunteer in Seattle, Washington. Around that same time, I met Dale Borglum, director of the Living/Dying Project in San Francisco. Dale started the Project in 1981 to address the urgent need for compassionate care for people dying from AIDS. I attended Dale's workshop in 2002 and have continued to support the project ever since.

When I started volunteering with hospice, I thought the work would give me the opportunity to talk with people about death and to share my own insights and experiences. I imagined myself as a kind of spiritual guide or mentor for the dying. My very first client disabused me of this notion from day one. He had no interest in talking about death, nor did he want a spiritual mentor. What he really wanted was someone to clean his apartment and take out the garbage. As I was vacuuming his apartment and fixing a plugged drain under his bathroom sink, I couldn't help but appreciate the irony of the situation—one that provided a much-needed reality check.

I'm still a volunteer with hospice and feel privileged to have been with dozens of patients through their dying processes. A recent patient was a big man about my age and with a huge heart and a great sense of humor. We became close during our time together, talking openly and facing the unknown together. I feel fortunate to have shared those few precious months with him.

I believe this work has helped me become more simple, open, and authentic with others. When I opened myself to the reality of death, I began to feel both the pain of personal loss and the beauty of this final stage of life— one that we all will go through eventually. This evolution occurred naturally, without any intention on my part. I found it was enough to simply spend time with the dying, respond to their needs, listen to their experiences, and observe my own reactions. I knew

experience ourselves as physical bodies. Yet intuitively we know that we're something more, even if we can't find the words to describe it. Just being in the presence of someone who is dying can help us appreciate the mystery and beauty of this paradox.

Deathbed Experiences

After my father died, I made a point to sit quietly with his body and simply feel the silence in the room. It felt like he was still very much alive and present in the room. And then at some point, I felt he was gone. The change was palpable and made a lasting impression on me. My whole perception of dying became lighter and more transparent. I had the same experience after my mother died, and other people have told me about similar deathbed experiences.

Two other experiences stand out in my memory,

perhaps because of the family connections. I was with my uncle when he died in 2003. After the hospice nurses left, I was alone in the house with his body. The funeral home was not scheduled to collect the body until the next morning. It didn't feel right to leave him in the house alone, so I decided to spend the night in the guest bedroom.

I awoke around 5:00 a.m. and remained in bed for a while with my eyes closed. Suddenly I became aware of choral music. I know this sounds like a cliché from a B movie. Nevertheless, the music was clear and unmistakable, like the sound of a women's choral group without words or instruments. When I opened my eyes and sat up in bed, the music went away. But as soon as I lay down and closed my eyes, I could hear it again. I did this several times and realized that I could tune my awareness to the music as if it existed on a certain bandwidth of consciousness.

I don't know the significance of this experience, but I've read accounts of similar music heard by those attending at a deathbed.[10] Dr. Raymond Moody refers to these and other kinds of deathbed experiences as "shared death experiences."[11] It's as if a doorway is opened when someone dies and everyone nearby gets a blast of light from the other side.

A somewhat different kind of experience occurred in 2008 just after my father died. My father's face

he was in his mid-40s. I knew it was my father but had no memory of ever seeing him so young.

No words were spoken. He smiled, and I felt he was pleased that we had shared parts of our lives together. This also struck me as unusual because during his life, my father and I were not particularly close and often at odds with each other. We were like two strangers who happened to end up in the same family. But immediately when he smiled, I felt that our relationship was meaningful and good, exactly as it had happened.

These kinds of experiences give us a glimpse of the multidimensional universe around us. Individually, they're easy to dismiss and forget about. But the cumulative effect of many such experiences has produced a lasting change in my perspective. Around the time I turned 60, I noticed that the existential crisis around death that tormented me as a child had vanished. I'm not sure exactly when it happened. One day the problem just no longer seemed relevant. My concept of death had been replaced by the knowledge that *Beingness*—the presence behind our experience—does not and, in fact, cannot die.

Of course, I still have the reflexive kind of fear that arises in dangerous situations. However, the sense of dread about dying is gone. Instead, I look forward to death in a positive way, as a great adventure. By the same token, I no longer experience the same kind of grief after death of a loved one. I miss being with the person in physical form, but I don't think of them as being dead. As the philosopher, Pierre Teilhard de Chardin said, "We are not human beings having a spiritual experience; we are spiritual beings having a human experience."[12]

Life Beyond Death – the Website

One day in fall 2006, while coming out of meditation, I opened my eyes and happened to glance at a picture of Maharishi's teacher Guru Dev. I immediately had a strong impulse to share with others what I had learned about death and the afterlife. As strange as this sounds, it felt as if Guru Dev were saying, "You've been given quite a lot. Now go share it."

During the next few months, I began to organize my thoughts about what I had learned from my out-of-

I put the material aside for some time after I had finished writing, not really sure if or how I wanted to proceed. Aside from the fact that I had never published anything before, I was terrified of going public with such a deeply personal view—one that many people wouldn't understand or may even consider delusional. On the other hand, I believed that some people would benefit from it. But I had no idea how many.

One advantage of getting older is that I tend to become less concerned about what other people think. So eventually, I decided to publish the material and let the chips fall where they may. After educating myself about self-publishing, I settled on a website as the most practical way to reach a wide audience. In 2008 I hired a web designer and together we created the website *Life Beyond Death*, linking it to a wide range of search words such as "life after death," "life beyond death," and "afterlife."

To my surprise, the website was well received. Within a year, the number of visits increased to about 1,200 per month and the web statistics show that many people are reading most, if not all, of the content. The visitors come from all parts of the world but mainly from the US and other English-speaking countries, including the UK, India, Pakistan, and Australia. I am still receiving several inquiries each week from people asking for more information or clarification or simply expressing their appreciation for the material.

I'll close this chapter with some thoughts from the home page of *Life Beyond Death*. For those who might like to read the entire website, go to: www.lifebeyonddeath.org.

Life Beyond Death

"To die is different from what any one supposed, and luckier."
                                    Walt Whitman - *Song of Myself*

Worldwide, roughly 160,000 people die every day. That's almost 60,000,000 people a year. In another 80 years, nearly everyone alive today will be gone. It can happen at any time, to anybody.

Most of us live in denial, as if death will never come. But sooner or later, death comes to everybody. And with it come a number of urgent questions: What happen ...

ʂtage oɟ ɩɩɩe wɩɩɩ ᴅe overshadowed with fear and confusion.

Why wait until the end? Why not ask these questions now, while there's time to make a serious inquiry? You just may discover what Walt Whitman was alluding to—something wonderful and completely unexpected.

Endnotes – Chapter 7

[1] A. Bloom, *The Republic of Plato* (Basic Books, Second Edition; 1991), Book X, 614b–621b

[2] R. Moody, *Life After Life* (MBB, Inc., 1975, HarperOne, current edition).

[3] G. Ritchie, *Return From Tomorrow* (Chosen Books, 1978).

[4] R. Moody, *Paranormal: My Life in Pursuit of the Afterlife* (HarperOne, 2012).

[5] P. van Lommel, R. van Wees, V. Meyers, and I. Elfferich, "Near-Death Experience in Survivors of Cardiac Arrest: a prospective study in the Netherlands," *The Lancet*, 12/15/2001, DOI: https://doi.org/10.1016/S0140-6736(01)07100-8.

[6] A. Goswami, *The Self-Aware Universe* (Tarcher-Perigee, March 1995).

[7] Wikiquote contributors, "Max Planck" https://en.wikiquote.org/w/index.php?title=Max_Planck&oldid =2579866 (accessed August 31, 2019), Quotation from interview in *The Observer*, January 25, 1931; p. 17.

[8] V. Khanna, "A New Science of Consciousness," *Hinduism Today*, April-June 2017.

[9] Wikipedia contributors, "Cryonics," *Wikipedia, The Free Encyclopedia,* https://en.wikipedia.org/w/index.php?title=Cryonics&oldid=91 1025486 (accessed August 27, 2019).

[10] Barrett, Sir William, *Death-Bed Visions – The Psychical Experiences of the Dying* (Lulu Co., 2013; original publication, 1927), Ch. 5.

[11] R. Moody, *Glimpses of Eternity; An Investigation into Shared Death Experiences* (Rider, 2011).

[12] R. J. Furey, *The Joy of Kindness* (Crossroad, March 1993), p.138.

Darshan

In spring 1987, I began another chapter in my life. After 15 years of intense focus on a career, I finally had the time and resources to pursue my lifelong dream—to explore different traditions and meet living spiritual masters around the world. Even though I viewed Maharishi's teaching as the gold standard, I wanted to broaden my perspective and learn more about other traditions.

During the next 10 years, I attended hundreds of spiritual gatherings and retreats throughout North America, India, Europe, and Australia. The teachers I met ran the gamut in every respect. Some were advanced adepts with an exceptional depth of knowledge and experience. Others were less impressive or simply didn't resonate with me.

Occasionally, I met someone who stood head and shoulders above the rest—a genuine spiritual master.

The notion of a spiritual master is not well known in the West. In the East, however, the idea is rooted in cultural and spiritual traditions that go back thousands of years. In this context, a spiritual master is an enlightened sage who embodies the highest levels of spiritual attainment and human development. In most cases, these individuals have tremendous charisma and *shakti*, or spiritual energy, and the ability to transmit this energy to others through sight, touch, or speech. On paper, these notions are abstract and defy the logic of Western thinking. Yet in the presence of someone invested with these qualities, the concept takes on a living meaning and the experience can be life-changing. In India, this experience is called *darshan*.

The Sanskrit word *darshan* literally means sight or appearance and usually refers to a physical meeting with a saint or holy person. The word also suggests a blessing that is bestowed during such an encounter.[1] Darshan can also take place in the subtle dimensions, such as during prayer, meditation, or even a dream. In a more esoteric context, darshan represents a window or opening in consciousness, allowing a brief glimpse into higher dimensions of reality.

Mata Amritanandamayi (Amma)

Amma was born Sudhamani on September 27, 1953, in the small fishing village of Parayakadavu in the state of Kerala on the southwestern tip of India.[2] As a child, Sudhamani was raised in poverty and often subjected to physical and emotional abuse by her family. Because of her mother's poor state of health, many of the responsibilities for raising a large family fell on her shoulders and as a result, she was able to complete only a few years of formal education. Despite these hardships, she was extremely devout by nature and spent most of her free time meditating and singing devotional songs.

As she grew into a teenager, young Sudhamani began having mystical experiences of Lord Krishna and, later, *Devi,* or the Divine Mother. During these episodes, she would fall into states of *bhava samadhi*, or trances of devotional ecstasy and divine possession.

As Sudhamani's devotional fervor grew, she became increasingly dissociated from her physical body and surroundings. She slept very little, spending most of her nights in meditation or devotional singing. What little sleep she did take would be on the ground under the night sky.

Even though the phenomenon of bhava samadhi is known in India, Sudhamani's case stirred a great deal of controversy because of her young age, gender, and low caste. As her spiritual experiences matured, however, the local people accepted her as a genuine saint. She became known as "Amma," or mother, and her following in the region grew.

In 1981, her devotees founded Mata Amitanandamayi Math to serve the needs of the people in South India. Since then, the organization and the scope of its outreach has continued to expand. Today, Amma leads a global network of humanitarian organizations to address the most basic needs in the world's poorest communities.[3] In addition, Amma tours the world each year, teaching and giving darshan freely to people on every continent.

I first met Amma in 1987 at Unity Church in Seattle. She was nearing the end of a North American tour and

Even though Amma was not well known in the US, she had gained a reputation as the "hugging saint," because of her unique style of giving darshan by hugging people one by one. When I first heard about this, it didn't seem all that unusual. I thought, "Isn't that nice? She gives out hugs." But when I learned that she routinely sits on a stage giving hugs to thousands of people for as long as 15 hours at a stretch without a break, I realized that this was no ordinary saint and no ordinary hug.[4]

Out of respect and more than a little curiosity, Anne and I set aside the afternoon and drove to the church. About 150 people showed up for the event, which at the time seemed like a good turnout. I realize now how fortunate we were to be with Amma in such an intimate setting. Her public events today are attended

by thousands of devotees who travel from all parts of
the world to receive darshan.

Soon after we arrived, Amma walked in followed by
three attendants. Immediately the room became quiet
and we all stepped aside with hands folded in *pranam,*
the traditional Indian salutation of respect and
reverence. A young woman suddenly screamed.
Without a word, Amma embraced the woman, who at
this point was simultaneously laughing and sobbing.
Everyone, including the attendants and even the
woman herself, seemed completely taken by surprise.
Then Amma moved on to the stage as if nothing had
happened. All of this took place in a matter of seconds,
leaving everyone bewildered. And yet for me, there
was something familiar about it. Having spent time
with Maharishi, I knew all too well that strange and
unexplained things frequently occur around a spiritual
master. It's just part of the territory and there's no use
in trying to figure it out.

The next hour consisted of a discourse on *bhakti yoga,*
or the path of love, given by one of Amma's attendants.
Occasionally, he would lead the group in *bhajans,* or
traditional Hindu devotional singing. At the time, I
considered *bhakti* somewhat inferior to *jnana,* the path
of knowledge. Nevertheless, I enjoyed the discourse

and participated in the bhajans, all of which went on for about 90 minutes. Then it was announced that

quickly. I knelt and before I had time to even look up, Amma's powerful arms pulled me into her bosom. At the time, I weighed 170 pounds and was in the prime of my strength. Yet I felt like a rag doll in Amma's embrace. My face was pressed into her shoulder, so I couldn't see anything. I felt myself being rocked while she sang in my ear, "Ma, Ma, Ma, Ma..." Something inside of me let go and I fell into a spacious awareness, while "Ma, Ma, Ma..." washed over me in waves of love. All the wounds of a thousand years seemed to dissolve and I became light as a feather. The next thing I remember was walking around outside the auditorium in a blissful daze, having just been hugged by the Mother of the Universe.

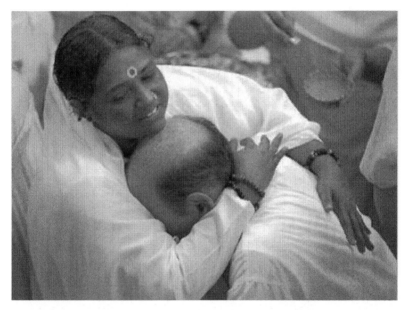

Mata Amritanandamayi (Amma), (1953-present); courtesy of M.A. Center, San Ramon, California

I believe that darshan with Amma gave me a direct experience of *bhakti,* the path of love. Plato pointed out in several of his dialogues that the intellect reaches only so far, but that love reaches to the highest realms. Meeting Amma helped me gain a deeper understanding of what he meant. Until that point in my journey, my questions had been Who am I? Why are we here? What does it mean to live a good life? After my encounter with Amma, a new question appeared on the horizon—How can I be of service? This marked

the beginning of a shift in my journey that is still
unfolding today.

ᴄᴇᴨᴛᴜᴿy ᴴⁱⁿᵈᵘ saint ana rounder ot Vedanta, with
whom he shares the same birthday.[5]

Ravi studied under Sudhakar Chaturvedi, a famous
Indian historian, Vedic scholar, social activist, and
former associate of Mahatma Gandhi during India's
struggle for independence.[6] As of this writing,
Chaturvedi is 121 years old and purported to be the
oldest living person in India. Young Ravi studied
science and the principle Vedic scriptures, many of
which he learned to recite by heart. This was the
beginning of his love for Vedic literature and science,
which eventually led to his close association with
Maharishi Mahesh Yogi.

In fall 1975, Ravi earned a BS degree in Physics from
Bangalore University. Around the same time, he
learned Transcendental Meditation (TM) and went on
to attend advanced TM retreats and training courses.

Sri Sri Ravi Shankar, October 1991,
Bangalore, South India;
courtesy of Dr. Eberhard Baumann

It was at one of these gatherings that Maharishi noticed young Ravi and asked him to join his organization. He

As much as Ravi appreciated the opportunity to work closely with Maharishi, the impersonal and often bureaucratic nature of a large organization did not resonate with his heart. In 1980, he decided to leave Maharishi and devote himself to another vision. There are different versions as to what prompted this breakup. One point on which everyone seems to agree is that Ravi felt pulled to a life of service and personal contact with students. These were desires he would never be able to fulfill in Maharishi's large organization, which focused primarily on the validation and promotion of TM.

In 1982 during a 10-day silent retreat, Ravi received the inspiration for a new spiritual practice that he called Sudarshan Kriya Yoga—a rhythmic breathing technique followed by meditation. He was quoted as saying that the practice, "...came to me like a poem, an inspiration. I learned it and started teaching it."[8] He began to attract students almost immediately. Most people who learned the practice were enthusiastic about the benefits, reporting increased calmness and clarity, greater physical energy, and a more positive outlook. As his following grew, his students began calling him *Guriji*, a title of respect and endearment.

A second and equally important part of Guruji's work is *seva*, or social activism and service. Toward this end, he founded the Art of Living Foundation, a volunteer-based organization focused on service and the promotion of peace and nonviolence. Currently, the foundation offers prison programs, peace initiatives, and interfaith programs to promote dialogue and cooperation among different religious groups.

I first learned Sudarshan Kriya Yoga in 1992. The practice takes about 20 minutes. I've found that it balances my physiology and enhances my experience in meditation. Also, when I do the practice in the morning, I seem to have more energy during the rest of the day. A year or so after I learned the practice, I attended a one-week advanced meditation retreat in Pittsburg, Pennsylvania, led by Guruji. There were about 80 participants and during the week, we had

many opportunities to be with Guruji in a variety of
settings.

had not shared with anyone who could have prepared
him. I had the feeling he was looking through me. This
could have seemed invasive or even frightening from
anyone else. But from Guruji, it felt completely
innocent and natural. His personality and energy
convey warmth and a genuine interest in each
individual.

For several hours each day during the course, Guruji
led us in several different practices designed to help us
experience the nature of consciousness and the body-
mind connection. None of these practices seemed
particularly exceptional at face value. Yet almost
everyone on the course experienced profound healings
and breakthroughs in their practice. Of the hundred or
more retreats I've attended, this one stands out as one
of the most powerful and unusual. I have no doubt that
Guruji's presence was the catalyst for the energy that
flowed out to the group that week.

During the 1990s, I spent time with Guruji in Vancouver, British Columbia, and in Seattle, Washington. He's an eloquent speaker—always casual, unscripted and innocent in his remarks. He manages to hold the audience in rapt attention. When speaking in public, he usually invites questions from members of the audience. At a Seattle event, one woman stood up and asked a question about Mary Magdalene and her relationship with Jesus. Initially Guruji was somewhat apologetic, saying that as a Hindu, he really didn't know anything about Mary Magdalene. There was a moment of awkward silence and I felt embarrassed for him, dangling alone on the stage.

Then Guruji did something unexpected. He said that he would look inside and see what came out of "the absolute." He closed his eyes for a few moments. When he opened them he began speaking and without hesitation delivered an eloquent discourse on Mary Magdalene, her relationship with Jesus, and how her influence shaped his teaching. I have no idea of its accuracy, but the woman who asked the question seemed deeply moved by his answer.

Something similar happened when I met with Guruji in a small group the next day. One woman in the group was suffering from a serious illness. She was seeing various doctors and the outlook was not good. When she asked Guruji for his help, he closed his eyes for a

the remarkable events that routinely occur around spiritual masters—incidents that most people would consider miraculous. Guruji never makes a show of these abilities, but neither does he hide them if they seem appropriate to the situation. This quality of naturalness seems to be ingrained in his personality, along with simplicity, openness, and friendliness towards others. Like Maharishi, these are not qualities that he teaches so much as consistently demonstrates in his behavior. I have found that this quality of "walking the talk" is a hallmark trait of a spiritual master.

Sri Ramana Maharshi

Ramana Maharshi was born as Venkataraman on December 30, 1879, in the village of Tiruchuli about 30 miles south of Madurai in Tamil Nadu, South India. He was the second of four children in a traditional

Hindu Brahmin family. By all appearances, he was a normal boy except for two unusual traits. He had near perfect recall after hearing or reading something for the first time. He used this talent in his studies and to memorize traditional Tamil poetry and scriptures. In addition, he was an unusually deep sleeper. Once he was asleep, it was nearly impossible to wake him by any means. Later he said that this was due to yogic practices from a previous lifetime. These habits still clung to him during his childhood, causing him to fall into *samadhi*, or deep absorption.

At the age of 16, young Venkataraman experienced a spontaneous awakening triggered by the contemplation of his own death. At the time, he was alone in his uncle's house in Madurai. Suddenly, for no apparent reason, he was overcome by the fear of impending death. Years later, Ramana described the event as follows:

> About six weeks before I left Madurai for good, a great change took place in my life. It was quite sudden. I was sitting alone in a room in my uncle's house, when a sudden fear of death overtook me. There was nothing in my state of health to account for it. I just felt, 'I am going to die' and I began thinking about it. The fear of

death drove my mind inwards and I said to
myself mentally, 'Now that death has come,
what do...

...with the death of this body am I dead? Is this
body 'I'? I am the spirit transcending the body.[9]

All of this was not dull thought, but flashed
through me vividly as living truth, which I
perceived directly, almost without thought
process. 'I' was something very real, the only
real thing about my present state, and all the
conscious activity connected with my body was
centered on that 'I.' From that moment onwards,
the 'I' or Self focused attention on itself by a
powerful fascination. Fear of death had vanished
once and for all. Absorption in the Self
continued unbroken from that time on.[10]

Ramana left home soon after this experience and
traveled to Mt. Arunachala, a place long known for its
spiritual power and as a hermitage for yogis and
siddhas, or spiritual adepts. For the next 20 years,

Ramana lived alone in silence, relying on others to look after his bodily needs. Gradually, an *ashram*, or spiritual community, gathered at the foot of Mt. Arunachala, where Ramana lived and gave darshan until his death in 1950.

Ramana Maharishi was a classic example of an *avadhut,* or extreme renunciate. The word is derived from the Sanskrit root "to shake" and usually refers to *sadhus* or holy persons who have shaken off the world. Avadhuts are mystics, saints, and often gurus, recognized for their radical state of freedom from conventional life. They typically roam freely, wearing little or no clothing, sleeping on the ground, and maintaining no visible means of support. In India, avadhuts are highly revered as saints of extraordinary spiritual power. Wherever they go, people seek their darshan and make every effort to feed and care for them in the hope that they will remain accessible and not disappear into the forest.

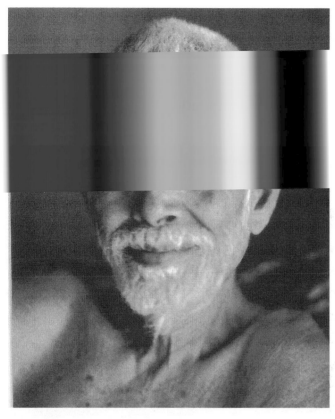

Ramana Maharishi (1879-1950);
courtesy of Ramanashramam,
www.sriramanamaharshi.org

My darshan with Ramana Maharishi occurred in 1994,
during my third trip to India. I realize it must sound
strange to hear about darshan from a saint who has
long since passed away. But for anyone who has spent
time at Ramanashram, such a story is perfectly
understood.

As Anne and I were planning a trip to explore the state of Tamil Nadu, several friends urged us to visit Ramanashram. I knew very little about Ramana Maharshi and didn't really believe all the stories about the spiritual power of Mt. Arunachala. Nor did I see much value in visiting the ashram of a saint who had died 44 years earlier. But my friends were insistent, so we decided to include Ramanashram on our itinerary.

I became seriously ill on the way to the ashram and by the time we arrived, I was weak and had a painful cough. As soon as we got to our room, I just wanted to lie down. But for some reason, I decided to go with Anne to the old meditation hall. When we sat down, I leaned up against the wall and closed my eyes, hoping to get some rest.

After a few minutes, I became aware of a light in my face. I opened my eyes and saw that the room was dimly lit. I closed my eyes again and soon the sensation returned. After this happened several times, I left my eyes slightly open, hoping to catch a glimpse of what was happening. This time I sensed the brightness in my peripheral vision as if the light were behind me. I looked overhead and out the window behind me, trying to figure out what was going on. This went on for about 10 minutes—playing cat and mouse with a strange light that crept over me whenever I relaxed my attention. Apparently, no one

his head tilted slightly and with a beatific smile. (See photo above.) I closed my eyes and soon the sensation of brightness came over me again. By now I was too exhausted to figure it out. I just accepted it and let go. Then I realized that the light was coming from *inside*. My whole being was flooded with light, along with a strong sense of Ramana's presence.

I opened my eyes and saw Ramana looking down at me from the picture. Unexpectedly, the question arose, "When I die, how will I find you?" I remember thinking that this was an odd question—one that had never occurred to me before. Yet for some reason, it came over me with great urgency, as if it were the only question in the world. Then I heard a voice ask in return, "How did you find me now?" In that moment, I had a clear experience of Ramana's darshan, entering my heart like a beam of light from higher dimensions of consciousness. I realized that his darshan is always available, here and now, beyond the cycles of life and death.

For the next few days, I had nagging doubts about this experience. Perhaps it was just a delusion triggered by the fever. But I heard similar accounts from other visitors, some even more dramatic than my own. Since then, I've read stories about Ramana appearing in people's dreams, even before they knew who he was. It was only later when they saw his picture that they recognized him as the man who appeared in their dream.

A common lament among spiritual seekers is that we were born too late, that all the great masters have come and gone. After having this experience at Ramanashram, I can see the mistake in this way of thinking. It's never too late. As fantastic as it sounds, I believe that the great masters are still alive and active in the higher spiritual dimensions and that their darshan is always available through the love that connects us to these higher planes.

Annamalaiyar Temple, South India

Temple represents the fire element in this tradition.

The Annamalaiyar Temple complex is one of the largest and most intricate in all of India. The complex covers 25 acres surrounded by a massive perimeter wall and four main *gopurams*, or tower gates, reaching 217 feet high. Inside the main walls, a series of inner compounds contain a vast network of hallways and inner sanctums, each lined with intricately carved pillars and overhead beams. The main temple construction began in the 9th century; additions were completed in the 14th and 16th centuries.[11]

Annamalaiyar Temple, as seen from Arunachala hill,
Tiruvannamalai, Tamil Nadu[12]

One could spend weeks exploring the temple complex
with its numerous shrines, *madapams* (pavilions), and
thousand-pillared hallways. It's an amazing
achievement of architecture and engineering built with
human hands using only ropes, pulleys, chisels, and
elephants to move the massive stones.

Walking through these corridors is a thrilling
experience. Traditional daily worship has been taking
place within the various shrines for more than 11
centuries. Just as the walls are caked with

accumulated soot from incense and butter lamps, the
atmosphere is equally laden with the reverberation of

varying in height from a few inches to several feet.
Because of its black abstract shape, the lingam
symbolizes the formless nature of Absolute
Consciousness, of which the world is an outward
manifestation. Traditional worship of the lingam
involves ritual bathing followed by anointment with
ghee, sacred ash, and garlands while a Brahmin priest
chants the prescribed prayers and thousand names of
Shiva. Afterward, the lingam is marked with the
traditional *tripundra*, or "three marks," consisting of
three horizontal stripes of sacred ash with a red dot of
kumkum, a bright red powder made of turmeric,
saffron, and lime. The tripundra is the sacred mark of
Shiva often seen on the foreheads of priests and
monks and over doorways as a reminder of God and
the sacred purpose of all life.

Shiva Lingam with tripundra.[13]

Even though I had been to the Annamalaiyar Temple half a dozen times, I had never attended *puja* (ritual prayer and offerings) there until 2009 when I was staying at Ramanashram with Anne and an old friend. The three of us arrived at the temple in early evening and saw a large crowd lined up outside the main complex. Apparently, this was a special festival puja because the long queue stretched from the temple entrance through the main courtyard and around the inner perimeter. We went to one of the many vendors and purchased our *prasad*, or offerings, consisting of baskets filled with fruit, flowers, and small packets of

rock sugar, sandalwood, and kumkum. We then
~~ ~~~~~~d~d t~ th~ r~ar ~f th~ q~~~~.

ΙΙΟΟΡΙΙαΙΙΙ.y ιɔ ս⊆⊆ρɪy ̣̣̣̣̣̣̣̣.........
everyone encouraged us to use the VIP line. We
accepted our visitor status and moved to the express
lane.

As we entered the temple, the atmosphere became
supercharged with energy. Our queue merged with
queues from other directions, forming a massive sea of
humanity moving toward the same goal—a brilliantly
lighted area about 50 yards ahead. The din of ringing
bells, the blare of trumpets, the pressure of a thousand
people being pressed into a tight space combined to
create an atmosphere of utter chaos.

As we got closer, we could see a flurry of activity
inside the inner sanctum where three Brahmin priests,
stripped to the waist and beaded with sweat, were
working furiously. The priest on the right was quickly
taking baskets and segregating the different offerings
into huge piles around the Shiva lingam. The priest in

the middle was ringing a large bell and chanting the holy names of Shiva while performing *arati*, the offering of light from burning camphor. The priest on the left was handing blessed offerings back to the devotees as they exited. The whole process was happening quickly, allowing each person about 10 seconds to receive darshan in front of the lingam before being ushered off to the left.

The clanging of the bell, the chanting of the priest, the smell of camphor, and the sound of a thousand hushed voices merged into a seamless drone. As I approached the inner sanctum, I felt my awareness pulled up and out of my body, caught in the grip of a powerful energy radiating from the inner sanctum. Then, in a matter of moments, I was back in my body and staggering to the exit with my companions. We made our way outside and looked at each other, stunned and with huge grins. The only words we could manage were, "Wow! Did you feel that?" I can appreciate why the Annamalaiyar Temple represents the fire element among the Shaivite temples of South India. We felt as if we'd been transported to the outer edges of the sun and back.

Prior to this experience, I considered ritualized worship purely in cultural terms as the natural extension of

mythology and tradition. Since then, I've come to see
these practices in a very different light. The

spiritual technologies ... g
communication between different dimensions of
consciousness.

Endnotes – Chapter 8

[1] The Yogic Encyclopedia, *Darshan*, Ananda Church of Self-Realization; https://www.ananda.org/yogapedia/darshan/ (accessed September, 14, 2019).

[2] S. Amritaswarupananda, *Ammachi: A Biography of Mata Amritanandamayi* (San Ramon, California: M.A. Center, 1994).

[3] Wikipedia contributors, "Mata Amritanandamayi," *Wikipedia, The Free Encyclopedia,* https://en.wikipedia.org/w/index.php?title=Mata_Amritanandamayi&oldid=911330463 (accessed August 27, 2019).

[4] J. Halpern, "Amma's Multifaceted Empire, Built on Hugs," *The New York Times*, May 25, 2013.

[5] Wikipedia contributors, "Ravi Shankar (spiritual leader)," *Wikipedia, The Free Encyclopedia,* https://en.wikipedia.org/w/index.php?title=Ravi_Shankar_(spiritual_leader)&oldid=912406972 (accessed August 27, 2019).

[6] Wikipedia contributors, "Ravi Shankar (spiritual leader)."

[7] M. Fischman, *Stumbling into Infinity: An Ordinary Man in the Sphere of Enlightenment* (Morgan James Publishing, October 2010).

[8] Wikipedia contributors, "Ravi Shankar (spiritual leader)."

[9] L. Narain (Ed), *Face to Face with Sri Ramana Maharshi* (Hyderabad, India; Sri Ramana Kendram, 2005).

[10] A. Osborne (Ed), *The Teachings of Ramana Maharshi* (Reprint by Ryder, 2014).

[11] Wikipedia contributors, "Arunachalesvara Temple," *Wikipedia, The Free Encyclopedia,* https://en.wikipedia.org/w/index.php?title=Arunachalesvara_Temple&oldid=912428853 (accessed August 27, 2019).

[12] Wikimedia Commons contributors, "View over Arunchaleshvara Temple from the Red Mountain - Tiruvannamalai - India 01.JPG," *Wikimedia Commons, the free media repository,* https://commons.wikimedia.org/w/index.php?title=File:View_over_Arunchaleshvara_Temple_from_the_Red_Mountain_-_Tiruvannamalai_-_India_01.JPG&oldid=269620931 (accessed August 27, 2019).

[13] Wikimedia Commons contributors, "File:Shiva Lingam at Shilparamam Jaatara.JPG," *Wikimedia Commons, the free media repository,* https://commons.wikimedia.org/w/index.php?title=File:Shiva_Lingam_at_Shilparamam_Jaatara.JPG&oldid=259928211 (accessed September 29, 2019).

A Higher Power

When I was in high school, I read *The Little Prince* by Antoine de Saint-Exupéry. One passage in particular struck a chord in me:

> And now here is my secret [said the fox], a very simple secret: It is only with the heart that one can see rightly. What is essential is invisible to the eye.[1]

When I began this journey in 1969, I had an intuitive sense of this invisible essence and was determined to find it. I studied teachings and learned spiritual practices from all over the world. I consumed volumes of esoteric knowledge and had many wonderful experiences. Yet after years of seeking, I was left with many of the same questions that I had in the beginning. I had to accept the basic ignorance and helplessness of my condition. Whatever power was needed to penetrate this mystery, I didn't have it.

The Quest for Enlightenment

The original Eastern concept of enlightenment has been considerably watered down by western culture. The word is often used to convey a spiritual awakening—a sudden and direct recognition of pure consciousness, or spirit, as one's true essential nature. Before the 1960s, this experience was rare in the West. It's more common today, primarily because of influences from the East. Nevertheless, in almost all cases, the experience represents a temporary opening or expansion of consciousness.

When I hear the term enlightenment used this way, I'm reminded of Mark Twain's quip about smoking: "Giving up smoking is the easiest thing in the world. I know because I've done it thousands of times."[2] By the same token, I would say that getting enlightened is also easy. It's staying enlightened that's tricky.

I don't want to diminish the importance of the awakening experience. The recognition of our spiritual nature is an important milestone and one that has altered the course of human evolution. But it's a peak

experience, lasting a few minutes, hours, or days at
ᵗʰᵉ ᵐᵒˢᵗ Eventually the experience fades and

or liberation. In this spe...
a release from both the bondage of ignorance and the
repetitive karmic cycle of birth, death, and rebirth.

The renowned spiritual master Ramana Maharshi
spoke about enlightenment in terms of the dissolution
of the *aham-vritti*, or "I" thought, which can be
equated to the egoic mind or sense of oneself as an
independent agent. Ramana sometimes used the term
mano-nasa (extinguished mind) to denote the
permanent dissolution of the "I" thought. On other
occasions he used the term *mano-laya* (subsided
mind) to denote its temporary abeyance.[3] [4] The
famous Bengali saint Ramakrishna Paramahansa
echoed this view when he said the following:

> How few are they who attain samadhi
> [absorption] and rid themselves of this *aham* ['I'
> thought], this self. It seldom goes. Reason as
> you will, discriminate without ceasing, still this

aham comes back to you again and again.
Today cut down the *Pepul* tree, but tomorrow
you will see it has sprouted forth again.[5]

Another sage, U.G. Krishnamurti, referred to the
enlightened as "goners."[6] I think this one word says it
all.

From these and other traditional descriptions, it's clear
that enlightenment in this permanent sense is an
extremely rare event. After nearly 50 years of seeking
out enlightened individuals, I've met only a very few
who, in my opinion, fall into this category.

Self-Power vs. Other-Power

Ramana Maharshi frequently said that essentially,
there are only two paths to enlightenment—*jnana
marga*, the path of knowledge, and *bhakti marga*, the
path of surrender.[7] As a general rule, he recommended
the path of knowledge, using the practice of self-
inquiry. This was his own path and the one he knew
from personal experience. As an alternative for those
not suited to self-inquiry, he recommended surrender
to a higher power. Sri Ramakrishna said as much
when he gave this advice:

If after all you cannot destroy this 'I,' then let it
~~~~~~ ~~ 'I the servant.' By acquiring the

enlightenment ~~~~~~~ , ~
Jodomon, the way of the Pure Land. The Holy Way is
called the path of wisdom, which can be attained only
through self-discipline and spiritual practices. For this
reason, the Holy Way is called the way of "self-power."
However, for those unable to follow the path of wisdom,
the Shakyamuni Buddha offered an alternative
approach—the Pure Land, which is a path of faith and
surrender to a higher power. For this reason, Pure
Land is called the way of "other-power."[9]

During my early life as a spiritual seeker, I believed
wholeheartedly in the way of self-power. It appealed to
my Western sense of independence and self-
determination. My efforts were not entirely in vain. I
experienced many profound awakenings to the
timeless, pure consciousness that transcends the mind.
Some of these awakenings lasted days or even weeks.
Invariably, they proved to be temporary just as Sri
Ramakrishna predicted. The egoic mind would reassert

itself, and the direct living experience of spirit would shrink into a memory.

Over the years, the rollercoaster ride of getting it and losing it eventually led to the realization that the path of self-power contains a fundamental flaw. The whole approach is rooted in the egoic mind—the very "I" thought that eventually must be transcended. Self-power is like a man sawing away at the branch of a tree on which he's sitting. Ultimately, I had to accept that enlightenment is not something I can do for myself. It can only be done for me.

All this occurred to me one night as I was reading in bed. Suddenly I became aware that my heart was beating, my gut was digesting, my lungs were breathing, my mind was thinking, the breeze was blowing, the geckos were chirping, and I didn't have control over any of it. Nor did I have the slightest idea how any of it was happening. All I could do was witness it. Then two words arose and took root in my mind: "Something else." In other words, something else must be behind all of this. It's like when you're outside on a bright sunny day. You don't have to see the sun to know that it exists—that the light must be coming from some brilliant source. With this insight, a feeling of tremendous relaxation came over me.

Free Will

always been impressed by the people who dedicate themselves to the AA program. This book gave me a whole new way to understand the esoteric teachings of the East.

It occurred to me that the 12 steps are an example of revealed knowledge, or knowledge that comes as a direct insight from higher spiritual dimensions. I know from my own experience that this kind of knowledge is available to each of us when we're ready to receive it. In their moment of deepest despair, the founders of AA discovered that by working together through a process of introspection and surrender to a higher power, their sanity was restored. I realized that as a spiritual seeker, this is exactly what I needed—to have my sanity restored. How ironic that after years of studying esoteric teachings from far corners of the world, I was dumbstruck by a simple wisdom discovered by two alcoholics in Akron, Ohio.

The 12 steps extend far beyond substance addiction.
The basic affliction of humankind is a belief to which
we are all addicted—the notion that we are
independent agents with the power to do what we want.
One doesn't have to dig very deep to find the many
false assumptions on which this belief rests or to see
how it feeds our dopamine receptors in the same way
as do alcohol, drugs, gambling, and sex.

We can begin by looking at the bulwark of Western
civilization—the notion of free will. One can support
this idea by pointing out all the times we seem to do
what we want. But in the process, we ignore all the
times when we can't do what we want, get what we
want, or even think what we want. The main reason
that gambling casinos are so successful is that people
tend to remember all the times they won and forget the
times they lost. We make the same mistake in
assuming that we have free will. If we really investigate
the situation, it's clear that we can do what we want
only some of the time. Does it make sense to say that
we have free will but only some of the time? If you
think so, then let's examine free will from another
perspective.

Consider our breathing. It's happening whether we
want it to or not. We can't stop it for more than a

minute or two. In a similar way, the events of our lives
f-ldin- -lon- a trajectory that is not in our

internal world: we like to ....
over our thoughts and feelings. But if we do, would we
ever choose to have an unhappy thought or painful
feeling?

One could counter this argument by saying, "Yes, but
look at all the things I've accomplished." Then we
need to ask ourselves very seriously: What part did we
play in making these things happen? If we're honest,
we'll admit that our own efforts play only a small role
in a complex web of genetic, social, and environmental
factors that contribute to our success. The traditional
Buddhist term *pratitya samutpada* (dependent
origination) refers to the interdependence of
everything. A flower in the forest doesn't bloom
without a vast network of support from the entire
universe. The human mind can comprehend only a
small fraction of these influences.

For the sake of argument, let's concede that on some level, we can do what we want. If I want a cup of tea, I can go to the kitchen and make one. But where did that desire come from? The truth is that I have no idea where it came from or how it arose. The 19th century German philosopher Arthur Schopenhauer expressed this point eloquently when he said, "Man can do what he wants, but he cannot want what he wants."[11]

Of course, on the surface, the freedom of human will appears to be the obvious case. Without it seeming this way and very convincingly so, I'm not sure how the world would work. The circumstances of human life demand that we live as if we are independent free agents. The more I consider this so-called free will, however, the more difficult it is to locate, or to understand how it works as a causative factor in my circumstances. Like the end of a rainbow, it's always just out of reach. All I can say with certainty is that free will is not what it appears to be.

A Higher Power

So if we aren't running our lives or the world around us, who or what is? I believe this is the essential spiritual question. The founders of AA used the term Higher Power, not so much as an answer but as a placeholder for the question itself. This is a term

Ramana Maharshi also used on several occasions. For
example he said this in response to a question about

prattle, "I do, I act, I function"[12]

Or, when he wrote the following:

The Ordainer controls the fate of souls in
accordance with their past deeds. Whatever is
destined not to happen will not happen, try how
hard you may. Whatever is destined to happen
will happen, do what you may to stop it. This is
certain. The best course, therefore, is to remain
silent.[13]

All the great traditions have pointed to this truth in one
way or another since the beginning of time. It's the
perennial view that transcends all arguments about
duality vs. nonduality. We are not living life. Rather,
life is living us.

When I began this journey, I was determined to grasp the coveted prize of enlightenment by my own efforts. However, I've gradually come to believe that enlightenment is not something we can attain. It's something we can only receive. All we can do from our side is make ourselves available by opening our awareness in honesty, simplicity, and humility.

At several points in this journey, I've come full circle. Yet the discoveries have always seemed fresh and new. Perhaps we're not traveling in circles but in spirals. With this thought in mind, I'll close with the oft-quoted passage from T.S. Eliot:

> We shall not cease from exploration
> And the end of all our exploring
> Will be to arrive where we started
> And know the place for the first time.[14]

Dear reader, I thank you for sharing this pilgrimage with me. If you are seeking, may this story keep you company on your journey. And may you forever abide in the open spaciousness of the question.

Endnotes – Chapter 9

³ A. Osborne (Ed.), *The Collected Works of Ramana Maharshi* (London: Rider & Co, Fifth Edition, 1979), *Self-Enquiry*, Verse 4, *Upadesa Saram,* Verses 13–15.

⁴ Sri Ramana Maharshi, *Talks with Sri Ramana Maharshi* (Tiruvannamalai, TN; Sri Ramanasramam, Ninth Edition, 1979), entry for November 5, 1936, p. 231.

⁵ Sri Ramakrishna Paramahansa, *Sri Ramakrishna's Teachings, Part I* (Lohaghat, N. India: Advaita Ashrama, Mayavati, 1916), Verses 156-157.

⁶ L. Brawley, *Goner: The Final Travels of U. G. Krishnamurti* (Non-Duality Press, May 2011).

⁷ Sri Ramana Maharshi, *Talks with Sri Ramana Maharshi*, entries for February 4, 1935, p. 40; January 6, 1936, p. 115; February 5, 1936, p. 134; December 28, 1937, p. 405.

⁸ Sri Ramakrishna Paramahansa, *Sri Ramakrishna's Teachings, Part I*, Verse 158.

⁹ Sho-on Hattori, *A Raft from the Other Shore* (Tokyo: Jodo Shu Press, 2000).

¹⁰ W. Liquorman, *The Way of Powerlessness; Advaita and the 12 Steps of Recovery*; (Redondo Beach, California: Advaita Press, 2012).

[11] A. Schopenhauer, Konstantin Kolenda (Trans), *Essay on the Freedom of the Will* (Dover Publication, 2005).

[12] Sri Ramana Maharshi, *Talks with Sri Ramana Maharshi*, entry for June 19, 1936, p. 177.

[13] Sri Ramanashramam, "At Arunachala," https://www.sriramanamaharshi.org/ramana-maharshi/at-arunachala (accessed September 21, 2019).

[14] T. S. Eliot, *Four Quartets*, "Little Gidding," Part V (Mariner Books, 1968).

Made in the USA
Coppell, TX
05 May 2020